CONFLICT and COMMUNION

RECONCILIATION AND RESTORATIVE JUSTICE AT CHRIST'S TABLE

DISCIPLESHIP RESOURCES

P O BOX 340003 • NASHVILLE, TN 37203-0003

www.discipleshipresources.org

ISBN 0-88177-478-2
Library of Congress Control Number 2005934550

Hymn text excerpt from J. Ernest Rattenbury, *The Eucharistic Hymns of John and Charles Wesley* used by permission from the publisher, OSL Publications, Akron, Ohio.

Scripture quotations, unless otherwise indicated, are from the New Revised Standard Version of the Bible, copyright © 1989 by the Division of Christian Education of the Nation Council of the Churches of Christ in the USA. All rights reserved. Used by Permission.

CONFLICT AND COMMUNION: Reconciliation and Restorative Justice at Christ's Table. Copyright © 2006 Discipleship Resources. All rights reserved. No part of this book may be reproduced in any form whatsoever, print or electronic, without written permission, except in the case of brief quotations embodied in critical articles or reviews. For information regarding rights and permissions, contact Discipleship Resources, P.O. Box 340003, Nashville, TN 37203-0003; fax 615-340-1789.

Table of Contents

Contributor Biographical Information

William Johnson Everett taught Christian Social Ethics for over thirty years at St. Francis Seminary, Emory University and Andover Newton Theological School before retiring in 2001 to focus on writing, worship reform, woodworking, and projects in the area of ecology and restorative justice. He has written extensively on religion and society issues in Germany, South Africa, India, and the United States. Earlier works include *God's Federal Republic: Reconstructing our Governing Symbol* (Paulist, 1985) and *Religion, Federalism, and the Struggle for Public Life: Cases from Germany, India, and America* (Oxford University Press, 1997). His book, *The Politics of Worship* (United Church Press, 1999) laid the groundwork for development of the roundtable worship described in this volume. He is presently writing an eco-historical novel weaving together stories about the Cherokee Trail of Tears and South Africa's Great Trek.

Gayle Carlton Felton is an elder in the North Carolina Annual Conference. Her Ph.D. is in the history of Christianity and she has served on the faculties of Meredith College and Duke Divinity School. Gayle is the author of several books and numerous articles on various aspects of United Methodism and on the teaching ministry of the church. She was the writer of United Methodism's official interpretive documents on the sacraments, *By Water and the Spirit: A United Methodist Understanding of Baptism* and *This Holy Mystery: A United Methodist Understanding of Holy Communion*.

Larry M. Goodpaster served as a United Methodist pastor for thirty-two years in the Mississippi Conference prior to his election as a bishop in 2000. He is a graduate of Millsaps College in Jackson, Mississippi, and earned both his M. Div. and D. Min. degrees from the Candler School of Theology at Emory University in Atlanta, Georgia. Bishop Goodpaster is assigned to the Alabama-West Florida Conference and, among several general church responsibilities, serves as President of the Board of Directors of JUSTPEACE: Center for Mediation and Conflict Transformation.

Stephanie Anna Hixon Stephanie Anna Hixon is an ordained elder in the Central Pennsylvania Annual Conference of the United Methodist Church. She served congregations in pastoral ministry, Christian education, and music prior to her ministry as a member the general secretariat for the General Commission on the Status and Role of Women in the United Methodist Church (1991-2002). Highly skilled regarding the Church's response to sexual harassment, abuse, and misconduct, Stephanie has been an advocate, educator, consultant, and facilitator in severely conflicted situations. Stephanie received a professional certificate in Alternative Dispute Resolution from Hamline University School of Law in St. Paul, Minnesota, and is committed to ministries of dispute resolution and peacemaking. She currently provides staff support for JUSTPEACE Center for Mediation and Conflict Transformation in the United Methodist Church.

David Anderson Hooker is a minister in the United Church of Christ. He received his Masters of Divinity (M.Div.) at the Candler School of Theology at Emory University and his Juris Doctor (J.D.) degree from Emory University School of Law. For more than twenty years, he has been a mediator and conflict transformation specialist. He has taught courses and led numerous workshops for clergy and laity in conflict transformation, visioning and leadership communications. He is a member of the Board of Directors of JUSTPEACE, an Associate Professor at the Center for Justice and Peacebuilding at Eastern Mennonite University in Harrisonburg, Virginia, and Associated Faculty at the Institute for Church and Management (ICAM), a Lilly Foundation program of the Interdenominational Theological Center in Atlanta, Georgia.

Jan Love is the chief executive officer of the Women's Division, the national staff of United Methodist Women, a historic women's mission organization within the General Board of Global Ministries. Prior to her work as head of the Women's Division, Jan taught international relations for twenty-four years, twenty-two of these at the University of South Carolina in the Department of Political Science. Her Ph.D. in political science is from Ohio State University. She has written a number of articles and books on a range of topics. From 1975 to 1998, Jan represented the United Methodist Church on the Central Committee (i.e., board of directors) of the World Council of Churches and continued to serve in a variety of advisory roles after 1998. Across these years, she held a number of leadership positions. In 2000 the United Methodist Council of Bishops honored her at General Conference for her "exceptional leadership in ecumenical arenas."

Marcia McFee has preached, led worship, and taught countless workshops for local churches and regional conferences across the U.S., Europe, and Asia. Dr. McFee received a Master's of Theological Studies degree at Saint Paul School of Theology with a concentration in Preaching and Worship and a Ph.D. from Graduate Theological Union in Liturgical Studies with an allied field of Ethics. She received the Hoyt Hickman Award for scholarship in the study of liturgy and effective worship leadership. Marcia has been a professor and guest lecturer at six seminaries in the area of worship and was the North Texas Conference (UMC) Consultant on Worship & the Arts.   She is the author of *The Worship Workshop: Creative Ways to Design Worship Together* (Abingdon Press).

Thomas W. Porter, Jr. is the Executive Director of JUSTPEACE Center for Mediation and Conflict Transformation of the United Methodist Church. He is an ordained elder of the New England Annual Conference, a trial lawyer, and a teacher at Boston University School of Theology, in addition to being a professional mediator. After graduating from Yale University, he received an M.Div. degree from Union Theological Seminary and a J.D. degree from Boston University Law School. He studied mediation at Harvard Law School and Eastern Mennonite University. He served twenty-three years as chancellor of the New England Conference. He was a founding partner of the trial firm of Melick & Porter LLP in 1983 and has been a trial lawyer since 1974, representing religious institutions, universities, hospitals, professionals, nonprofit organizations, and others. He is a member of the Journal of Law and Religion and chaired it from 1989 to 2001.

Peter Storey is Williams Professor of the Practice of Christian Ministry at Duke Divinity School. A former Bishop in the Methodist Church of Southern Africa and President of the South African Council of Churches, he was deeply involved in the church struggle against apartheid, in the National Peace Accord structures that followed, and in the selection of the nation's Truth and Reconciliation Commission. His publications include *With God in the Furnace: Preaching Costly Discipleship* (Abingdon Press), and *Listening at Golgotha* (Upper Room Books).

Marjorie Thompson is an ordained Presbyterian minister who directs Pathways in Congregational Spirituality, a program of Upper Room Ministries in Nashville, Tennessee. She has been engaged in teaching and retreat work around personal and corporate spiritual practice for more than twenty years. The author of two books, including *Soul Feast*, she has also served as an architect and author for *Companions in Christ*, a series of small group resources in spiritual formation that shows signs of fostering a renewal movement among congregations of many denominations.

Introduction

As a trial lawyer, minister, and chancellor for twenty-three years for my annual conference, I became aware of the problems with the adversarial retributive system for dealing with conflict and harm. What I discovered is familiar to all of us, as I experienced this not only in the courtroom, but also in our churches, and in our communities. In fact, I began to see the adversarial retributive system of our courtrooms as the model for most of our practices in dealing with conflict and harm in this world. I have spent the last decade in search of a better way—a more constructive way, a way of living out our calling to be ministers of reconciliation. (2 Cor 5:17-19)

This journey has taken me from the courtroom to tables of conversation, dialogue, and mediation. Here I learned that engaging conflict and addressing harm has to do with relationships and working toward restructuring relationships, with the participants empowered to transform their own problems and conflicts. A significant part of the journey took place in South Africa studying the Truth and Reconciliation Commission. Here an understanding of the body of Christ came alive through the concept of *ubuntu:* we are who we are because of our relationships. When I dehumanize you, I dehumanize myself. We are interconnected and interdependent. I saw the power of the telling and hearing of stories. I witnessed the essential practice of forgiveness. I also discovered a new understanding of justice, restorative justice, which moves us from a narrow focus on punishing offenders to "a process to involve, to the extent possible, those who have a stake in a specific offense and to collectively identify and address harms, needs, and obligations, in order to heal and put things as right as possible."[1] The most recent part of the journey has been with the JUSTPEACE Center for Mediation and Conflict Transformation of the United Methodist Church, helping to develop the theology, theory, and practice of faith-based conflict transformation. Among the lessons from working with the church has been the power of the circle process: the recognition of sacred space through ritual, the creation together of relational covenants to guide how we treat each other, the use of a talking piece to give everyone voice and promote good speaking and good listening, and a circle of collective wisdom where everyone is equally responsible for the outcome.[2]

Early on I recognized the importance of getting people to a table where they could engage each other and work together to address the issues, the harm, and the problems that divide them. The interesting thing that happened to me on this journey was that the table to which I was drawn was the Table of Holy Communion. On this journey, I have developed a growing conviction that it is at the Table of Holy Communion that we will find the *place,* the *time,* the *ritual,* and the *spiritual power* for healing relationships and doing the work of reconciliation in this world. I have discovered wonderful companions on this journey, including the authors of the chapters of this book. Here together we explore this common conviction from a variety of perspectives and the reasons for this conviction. To begin our conversation I want to identify some of the reasons for this core conviction.

The essential principle is that the one who reconciles and heals is the host of this Table. The one in whom God was incarnate is present at all tables, but here at this Table, we recognize the host and consciously open ourselves to this one. This is the one that broke down the walls of hostility. (Eph 2:14) This is the one through whom God reconciled the world to God's self, not counting their trespasses. This is God's Table. This book asks the question: What if we truly opened our whole being to this power, to this Spirit that can transform our conflicts, heal our broken relationships and bring us together?

The reasons are made clear in the liturgy itself. We see that the liturgy of Holy Communion opens us up to the one who reconciles and heals. It forms us as peacebuilders, ministers of reconciliation. To this table God invites all who "seek to live in peace with one another."[3] The message is of God's forgiveness and steadfast love in spite of our failure to love God and neighbor. God invites us to "offer one another signs of reconciliation and love." Through the Great Thanksgiving we enter into God's salvation history of formation in God's image, liberation, and reconciliation—in order to be "one with Christ, one with each other, and one in ministry to all the world." Finally, we are dismissed to "Go forth in peace." Ritual is about spiritual formation. This book asks the question: What might we be for this world if we took this liturgy seriously and allowed ourselves to be formed into ministers of reconciliation?

No one at this Table is unaware of the destructive conflicts in our world, in our communities, in the workplace and in our homes. We bring all these conflicted worlds to the Table. The greatest issue of our day is how we are going to break out of the cycles of retribution and violence that are tearing our world and our relationships apart. At the Table of Holy Communion, each time we commune, we are reminded that the only way out of these cycles is through the path of forgiveness. At this Table we celebrate the defeat of the powers of retribution and violence through the Word of Forgiveness from the cross and through the resurrection. Here we finally are freed to give up the idolatry that violence is redemptive, that it will save us. This book asks the question: What transformation might we offer the world if at the Table and from the Table we led our communities on the path of forgiveness?

Most of us at the Table are not oblivious to the deep conflicts in our churches, with some of our conflict around the meaning of Holy Communion itself. Walter Brueggemann says, "It is around that table that we have had our greatest conflicts because we know intuitively that in eating and drinking we are choosing our brand of *shalom* and legitimating an ordering of our world."[4] In our church we find great divisions on a variety of issues to the point where some even talk of schism. One of the toughest problems in the work of conflict transformation is how to get people to the table who disagree. At the Table of Holy Communion, we all find ourselves standing together, regardless of our differences. I have a growing conviction that on some issues we are not, at least in the near term, going to find common ground, but we can find at the Table higher ground, transcendent ground to which we are invited and where we can stand together. We may not find common ground but we find in God's self-giving love the ground for our ultimate reconciliation. This book asks the question: What would the body of Christ look like for the world if we began to celebrate this gift and this reality?

What are some other reasons for the conviction that it is at the Table of Holy Communion that we will find the *place,* the *time,* the *ritual,* and the *spiritual power* for healing relationships and doing the work of reconciliation in this world? The Table is the table of the good news that we are reconciled with God and that we can be reconcilers. In United Methodism, we, with John Wesley, believe that Holy Communion is a converting ordinance, not merely a confirming ordinance.[5] We do not share in Holy Communion because of our worthiness.[6] We come out of our hunger to receive God's gracious love, to receive forgiveness and healing. It is not a reward for penance and merit but a means by which God transforms us more fully into God's image. It is a means of grace. The Table is the table of vulnerability where I can come "just as I am." The Table is a place where we can be authentic and truthful, where God knows us and "no secrets are hidden."[7] This sacred space becomes a safe space.

At this table, in the words of Walter Brueggemann, holiness is seen as "unanxious with the other engagement," not separation.[8] As John Wesley said, "The Gospel of Christ knows no religion but social, no holiness, but social holiness."[9] Here we understand our interconnection and interdependence. We need each other. The Table is a place of accountability to God, to each other, to the cosmos. It is a Table of restorative justice, of healing. The Table is a banquet table placed in the presence of our enemies. This is a Table of abundance, not scarcity, for the whole of the cosmos.

Is this the way, however, that we actually experience communion? Are we among those who try to avoid Holy Communion Sunday? Do we see the ritual as primarily food for me and not food for the community and the world? Do we experience it only as individualistic and self-serving, or truly as relational and communal? The first person pronouns throughout the liturgy are consistently plural—"we," "us," "our."[10] Part of Paul's condemnation of the eucharistic practices of the Corinthian church is that they do not wait for the rest of the community to gather and they do not share their food. (1 Cor 11:21, 33) Is our Table one of the most segregated and exclusive tables we experience in our lives? For United Methodists the Table is an open table, open to all. There is space for everyone and everyone is equal at the Table. This book will explore how Holy Communion comes alive as a Table of Healing, a Table of Restorative Justice, and a Table of Reconciliation.

The most important lesson for me about the Table has come through studying what Jesus did at the Last Supper, the meal we are called to remember. This has led to the conviction that the Table might become transforming and formative for us and for the world when we begin to recognize, with Jesus, that the Table is a place to name and engage our conflicts and practice reconciliation.

Jesus, at the Last Supper, names the conflicts in the room. He names the elephant in the room when he says, "[O]ne of you will betray me, one who is eating with me." (Mark 14:18b) He also names the whole conflictual system of his day by moving from the head of the table to the foot of the table and washing everyone's feet. (John 13:3-16) Finally, he notes that Simon Peter and the rest of the disciples will desert him. The naming is important. Justice requires the naming. Truth requires the naming. As important, transformation requires the naming. The naming also helps us understand the significance of the bread and wine. In the naming, we begin to see our need. We experience our hunger. We feel our thirst. We know we need God and each other. We need to be reconciled and to be a reconciler.

What Jesus does next is remarkable, radical, and transforming in the context of his day and ours. He does not give a stone, or retribution, or punishment. He gives bread and wine to Judas, to Peter, to everyone. Here Jesus reframed the reality of our world. Reality is not about retributive justice, but restorative justice. This act of giving bread and wine is the symbolic act of forgiveness written deep in the Last Supper.

We are called to do the same. I have come to believe that, if we can engage our conflicts at the Table in the context of Holy Communion, we will be present with Jesus, and Holy Communion will become the most powerful, healing ritual known to human kind, especially when we bring to the Table the lessons we have learned from the field of conflict transformation. This perspective on Holy Communion might be new to you, but it is grounded in Jesus' actions and teaching at the Last Supper. In this book we will begin a conversation about how we might practice reconciliation at the Table.

In this book we will also talk about actual tables that express these convictions. The table on the cover of this book is, for me, an example of such a table. The carpenter for this table was William Everett.[11] With Bill, as he explains in his chapter, I believe that round tables express the meaning of Holy Communion better than altars. The table is based on two arches supported by a circle of cherry that represents a well, a deep well of baptismal water. The water springs forth on the surface of the table in the mosaic, moving from white tiles to the multi-colored tiles of God's rainbow covenant with Noah. The water is flecked with red—drops of blood—recognizing the connection between our baptism and our experience of Holy Communion. From the water come four mandorlas, the most ancient of Christian symbols. A mandorla is created by the intersection of two circles, representing here the intersection of heaven and earth, experienced most clearly in Jesus the Christ. Early Christians added a tail to the mandorla and created the symbol of the fish. These mandorlas form a cross, which can be seen also as a budding flower and the four points on the compass. Inlaid in the first mandorla are sheaths of wheat made from poplar. In the second mandorla are grapes from purpleheart. In the third mandorla in holly wood is the dove of peace descending on the waters. Finally, in zebrawood is a feather, a talking piece in Native American communities, a symbol of good talking and good listening, indispensable to the practice of reconciliation at the table. Soon the table will be set and chairs will be brought for the guests. The word and the gift of reconciliation will be received and the ministry of reconciliation will be practiced at the Table.

The belief in the importance of Holy Communion found resonance in the action of the General Conference of the United Methodist Church through its adoption in 2004 of *This Holy Mystery: A United Methodist Understanding of Holy Communion.*[12] The General Conference has recommended that each church study the ritual of Holy Communion and practice it weekly. The United Methodist Church is moving closer to the practice of John Wesley who exhorted us to participate in the celebration of Holy Communion as often as possible.[13] This book is an affirmation of the importance of this action and an exploration of its meaning for the daily work of reconciliation.

An Episcopalian priest, who is a colleague, noted recently that Episcopalians have always celebrated communion weekly and he has not seen it make an appreciable difference in the spiritual formation and practice of his parishioners. He liked the idea of engaging our conflicts at the Table as a way of opening up the meaning and the formative power of the Table.

So, how does conflict inform Holy Communion and how does Holy Communion transform conflict?

On this journey to the Table, I have been inspired and guided by the individuals who have agreed to contribute to this book. With patience and wisdom they have each in different ways helped me experience a deeper understanding of Holy Communion.

In *The Last Supper: Naming the Conflicts and Giving Bread and Wine,* I explore more fully the words and actions of Christ at the Last Supper.

In the second chapter, *Holy Communion in the Life of the Church: The Theology and Experience of Reconciliation,* Gayle Felton presents the broad range of meanings and understandings laid out in *This Holy Mystery: A United Methodist Understanding of Holy Communion,* which she authored, and in United Methodist ritual as prelude to the more focused concern of reconciliation. In affirming the centrality of Holy Communion in the life of the church, she shows how Holy Communion is context and empowerment for forgiveness and reconciliation within and beyond the community of the church. This chapter will also present the challenge of making Holy Communion not only a part of our weekly worship, but also of the deep fabric of our lives and our mission in the world.

In the third chapter, *Holy Communion and the Vision of the Beloved Community*, Bishop Larry Goodpaster suggests that Holy Communion is the place where we as a church find the beloved community and where we can be the body of Christ in this deeply broken and conflicted world. He uses the story of David and the son of Jonathan to set the framework for understanding the world we live in as well as for understanding the meal that shapes the beloved community.

The essential theme of forgiveness is developed in the fourth chapter by Marjorie Thompson. *Communion and Forgiveness: Awakening to the Circle of Love.* Here she opens up the forgiveness we experience in receiving the bread and wine, and explores the journey of forgiveness to which we are called as followers of Jesus the Christ. This fourth chapter helps us to understand the central role of forgiveness in the liturgy and in our everyday lives.

Peter Storey contributes the fifth chapter, *Table Manners for Peacebuilders: Holy Communion in the Life of Peacemaking* focusing on the drama of the Holy Communion liturgy with its transformative potential for the lives of peacebuilders. In this chapter he explores how Holy Communion empowers us in the work of peacebuilding and how it models important steps in reconciliation.

In *Ritual Formation: Liturgical Practices and the Practice of Peacebuilding*, Marcia McFee helps us discover how our liturgical practices have the power to form and shape us. Here we see how ritual processes are necessary to deal with conflict, helping us navigate the "liminality" of broken relationships. This sixth chapter shows how dealing with conflict through circle processes of restorative justice can inform and reform our ritual practice of Holy Communion.

In the seventh chapter, *The Practice of Reconciliation at the Table,* I explore themes from the fields of conflict transformation and restorative justice, and how they might inform our practice of restorative justice and reconciliation at the Table. We look at some examples where such a practice has occurred, including actual steps in the process.

In the eighth chapter, Stephanie Hixon facilitates a further exploration of the practice of Holy Communion as a ritual that offers courage and hope in the midst of conflictual and broken relationships. *Holy Communion and the Healing of Relationships* revisits the themes of forgiveness, being reconciled and being called to be reconcilers, exploring some difficult questions about healing relationships, particularly in the context of sexual abuse. How do we experience the healing of relationships? What about those who have experienced seemingly unforgivable acts of violence or betrayal? Can and should those who have caused harm and those who have been harmed come together at table? In community we glimpse the wonder and despair of relationships intertwined with one another and with God. In the practice of Holy Communion, we open ourselves to the living and healing presence of God.

In the seventh chapter, *Grandma's Supper is the Lord's Supper: The Experience of African American Fellowship Meals and Sunday Supper as Communion,* David Anderson Hooker focuses us on the Table as the place for fellowship and a meal, a foretaste of the heavenly banquet. This chapter proposes a re-visioning of the *fellowship meal,* which is a primary act of African American (Black Church) community formation, as the time and venue in which to celebrate Holy Communion. The implications for both Holy Communion and fellowship meals for all of us will be explored here.

Practicing Consensus at the Table: Doing Democracy Differently , by Jan Love, shows how Holy Communion might inform and inspire our attempts at holy conferencing, and how our attempts at holy conferencing through consensus decision-making might make a reality of our being "one with Christ, one with each other, and one in ministry to all the world."[14]

In the final chapter, *Gathering at the Roundtable,* William Everett shows how the actual shape of the Table can make a difference in our understanding and experience of Holy Communion. The singular symbol of reconciliation in our world today is the roundtable, which came to expression in the revolutions in Poland and East Germany, and then has found repeated expression in South Africa, the United States and in other contexts that seek to move people from deep conflict to public peace. By putting a round table at the center of worship, we reshape our paradigms of right relationship, create a spiritual energy of mutuality and trust, and provide models for reconciliation in the world. He will report on the experience of his church at such a table.

Through these reflections we hope that together we can come to understand how conflict informs communion and how communion transforms conflict. We hope that we all find ways to place the Table of Holy Communion in the midst of the conflicts of our times. Through the practice of reconciliation empowered by the liturgy of Holy Communion, we hope that the Table will become for all of us and for our world a source of healing, transformed life, reconciled relationships, with God, and with one another.

Thomas W. Porter

Notes

1. Howard Zehr, *The Little Book of Restorative Justice* (Intercourse: Good Books, 2002), 37.

2. I will develop this journey and these learnings in Chapter 7.

3. From "A Service of Word and Table I," *The United Methodist Hymnal* (Nashville: The United Methodist Publishing House, 2004), 7.

4. Walter Brueggemann, *Peace* (Atlanta: Chalice Press, 2001), 78.

5. John Wesley, Journal from November 1, 1739, to September 3, 1741: Friday, June 27, 1940.

6. Gayle Carlton Felton, *This Holy Mystery* (Nashville: Discipleship Resources, 2005), 67. Wesley said that 1 Cor 11:27-32 does not apply to the people who are to commune, but to the manner in which the consecrated elements are consumed.

7. From "A Service of Word and Table I," *The United Methodist Hymnal* (Nashville: The United Methodist Publishing House, 2004) p. 6.

8. Walter Brueggemann, "Vision for a New Church and a New Century, Part 2: Holiness Become Generosity," *Union Seminary Quarterly Review. Vol. 54:2000)*: p. 54.

9. John Wesley, Preface to *Hymns and Sacred Poems*

10. From "A Service of Word and Table I," The United Methodist Hymnal, (Nashville: The United Methodist Publishing House, 1989) p. 6-11.

11. I am deeply indebted to Bill for many reasons, including his willingness to help shape the structure of this book and give editorial guidance on the essays, especially mine.

12. *The Book of Resolutions of the United Methodist Church* (Nashville: The United Methodist Publishing House, 2004), 884-931.

13. Felton, 65.

14. From "A Service of Word and Table I," The United Methodist Hymnal (Nashville: The United Methodist Publishing House, 1989), p. 10.

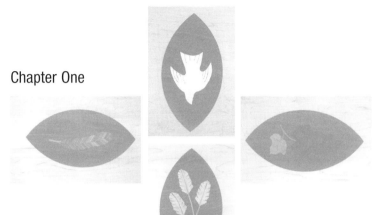

Chapter One

The Last Supper
Naming the Conflicts and Giving Bread and Wine

THOMAS W. PORTER

> *When it was evening, he came with the twelve. And when had taken their places and were eating, Jesus said, "Truly I tell you, one of you will betray me, one who is eating with me." They began to be distressed and to say to him one after another, "Surely, not I?" He said to them, "It is one of the twelve, one who is dipping bread into the bowl with me. For the Son of Man goes as it is written of him, but woe to that one by whom the Son of Man is betrayed! It would have been better for that one not to have been born." While they were eating, he took a loaf of bread, and after blessing it he broke it, gave it to them, and said, "Take; this is my body." Then he took a cup, and after giving thanks he gave it to them, and all of them drank from it. He said to them, "This is my blood of the covenant, which is poured out for many. Truly I tell you, I will never again drink of the fruit of the vine until that day when I drink it new in the kingdom of God." (Mark 14:17-25)*

The primary inspiration and guidance for these reflections on the relation between conflict and communion are the actions and words of Jesus at the Last Supper. This is the meal we are called to remember as we participate in Holy Communion. "Do this in remembrance of me." (Luke 22:19; 1 Cor 11:24-25) This is more than recalling. It is an anamnesis—a re-presentation. Christ is truly present. As with the disciples on the road to Emmaus, we recognize Jesus in the breaking of the bread. (Luke 24:13-35)

The Last Supper is a meal in the midst of conflict where Jesus names the conflicts in the room, and then gives bread, the gift of forgiveness, not a stone, or retribution, or punishment. In remembering this living reality, we are called to re-member or re-frame our world and our own actions so that we do likewise. This chapter will explore Jesus' words and actions at the Last Supper and their implications for our understanding of conflict transformation and Holy Communion.

Conflict: The Context of the Last Supper

During Passover

To set the stage, we know that this meal is related in some way to Passover and the remembrance of slavery and exodus from Egypt. We do not need to get into the debate as to whether this is actually a Passover meal in order to say that this meal occurred in the Passover season with all the meaning of this season. "Passover" relates to the action of God in passing over and smiting the first-born in Egypt (Exod 12:12) or passing over and sparing the "houses of the Israelites in Egypt." (Exod 12:27) The context was the enslavement of the people of Israel and their ultimate liberation or exodus. Significant conflict!

In Jerusalem

We also know that this supper takes place in Jerusalem. Jesus knows that there are religious and political forces in Jerusalem that want to kill him. He does not head for the hills, nor does he join the zealots to fight. In fact, he courageously enters the eye of the storm on a donkey.

In our churches, we know that the primary way of dealing with conflict is avoidance, "heading for the hills." In our world, we know that ultimately we take up the sword, believing that only violence will save us, that violence can be redemptive. Jesus rejects both flight and fight. He chooses a third way.

So the context of the Last Supper is conflict, recognized historically through the celebration of Passover and through the present reality for Jesus and his disciples in Jerusalem.

A Meal

Meals, times of nourishment, relationship, and communion, are key events in the life of Jesus. In many ways, he defines his ministry around meals and with whom he eats. He eats with sinners, with gentiles and tax collectors. His enemies noticed this. This was part of their complaint against him. Jesus created conflict by his eating habits. His table fellowship was a living parable of forgiveness.

His meals were banquets, recognition of the abundance of creation and the unlimited nature of love and nurture as seen in the feeding of the five thousand. This table of abundance is set in the presence of his enemies.

This is a meal at the end of a long journey for Jesus, similar to the journey in the twenty-third Psalm. Through the "darkest valley" he comes to the table in the midst of and in the presence of his enemies. This is ultimately a table of restoration and reconciling encounter and he gives a cup that overflows.

Here in the midst of the life and death conflict in which Jesus finds himself, Jesus moves to bring his disciples, including Judas, around him for one last supper. This is a table for a meal, not an altar.

Naming the Conflicts at the Table

After they have taken their places and are eating, what are the first words that we hear Jesus say? He says, "Truly I tell you, one of you will betray me, one who is eating with me." He added, "It is one of the twelve, one who is dipping bread into the bowl with me." (Mark 14:17-20) Isn't this startling? What a way to start a dinner party! The first words of Jesus, at his final dinner with his disciples, name the conflict that is the elephant in the room. Judas is going to betray Jesus.

We see in John's Gospel the other way that Jesus names the conflict in which he found himself, the conflict written deep into the whole social fabric of his day. He moves from the head of the table to the foot of the table, takes the place of the least and washes the feet of all the disciples. (John 13:3-17) In doing so, he names the structural and systemic problem of his society. He turned the society upside down. We are reminded of his response to the disciple who wants to know "Who is the greatest in the kingdom of heaven?" (Matt 18:1) Jesus responds by putting the child in the middle and saying that we must become like a child, the person with the least status of anyone in his society. In doing so, he says that life is not about striving for status. It is about being in relation to God and neighbor, as the great commandment says. The children are the ones whose "angels continually see the face of my Father in heaven." (Matt 18:10) The question of the disciples comes out of scarcity. It is a question that comes out of the anxiety created by striving. As Reinhold Niebuhr says, "Anxiety is the internal precondition of sin."[1] The child lives in abundance, experiencing life as a gift, experiencing humility as wonder looking into the face of God. These teachings threatened the power structures of his day to the point where the decision was made that he needed to be killed.

In John's Gospel, Jesus also names the denial and abandonment that he will experience. Peter, the one on whom the future church would be founded, asked, "Lord, why can I not follow you now? I will lay down my life for you." Jesus answered, "Will you lay down your life for me? Very truly, I tell you, before the cock crows, you will have denied me three times." (John 13:37-38) Jesus says in Mark, "You will all become deserters . . . " (Mark 14:27) Abandonment is what most of us do. We do not feel we need God. We do not have the courage to follow God's way.

There is nothing Pollyannaish or sentimental or individualistic or pietistic about this meal. The meal is not privatized or spiritualized. There is nothing here that is romantic or escapist. This is the real world, with real and deep conflict. So here Jesus sits at his last supper, under the shadow of the cross with the man who would betray him and eleven others who will desert him. Does that sound conflictual to you? And Jesus named it. Justice requires the naming. Truth requires the naming. As important, transformation requires the naming. What is unnamed lies just beneath the surface. It often develops dis-ease. It gets worse until it explodes in very destructive ways. You must name it to heal it. Diagnosis is necessary for treatment. The naming, for Jesus, was the only way to begin the process of transforming this conflict into something constructive, into a new covenant, into a new revelation. The naming also helps us to understand the significance of the bread and wine. In the naming, we begin to see our need. We experience our hunger. We feel our thirst. We know we need God and each other. We need to be reconciled and to be a reconciler.

Giving Bread and Wine

What Jesus does next is remarkable, radical, and transforming in the context of his day and ours. After naming the conflict, he turns and offers everyone—Judas, Peter, everyone—bread and wine. Think about this gesture. He reaches over to Judas and gives him a portion of a loaf that he has blessed, not cursed, and says to Judas, "Take; this is my body." He also gives this bread to Peter and all the others who would deny him. Then he takes a cup, and after giving thanks he gives it to them, and all of them drink from it—*all* means Judas as well as Peter. He says, "This is my blood of the covenant, which is poured out for many." (Mark 14:22-24)

The bread is the symbol of God's sustenance of God's creation best symbolized by the manna in the wilderness. The wine is a sign of the heavenly banquet. (1 Cor 11:23-26, Matt 26:26-29) It is a sign of the new covenant between God and God's people—a covenant of forgiveness and reconciliation. The one cup symbolizes the unity of the body in Christ gathered at the table.

Jesus names the conflict, but not in order to give a stone or to set the stage for retribution and punishment. He names it and then gives bread and wine. Indeed, he gives his life. Here Jesus reframes our whole reality and the way we are to respond to conflict, differences, and harm.

This is a different reality from the world of Judas and the reality of our world. This is a different way to deal with betrayal and harm. This is a different way of dealing with violence, where you name the harm and give bread to your enemy. You name the conflict and respond with the gift of forgiveness. Think of what he has done with bread and wine, whose ingredients have gone through a process of being beaten, ground, and trodden underfoot. This act of giving bread and wine is the symbolic act of forgiveness written deep in the Last Supper.

Reframing: Naming and Giving Bread and Wine

In the world of conflict transformation, we talk about the importance of reframing statements as well as issues and problems. The reframing takes seriously the issue or the problem, including the naming of it, but gives it a new perspective that opens up potentially more constructive possibilities. What Jesus does at the Last Supper is a profound example of this.

The frame within which the society of Jesus' day operated was the frame of naming for the purpose of punishment or retribution. The movement in Israel's Scriptures [the Old Testament or Hebrew Bible] is from the law of Lamech, retribution of seventy-sevenfold, (Gen 4:24) to proportional and limited retribution, an eye for an eye. (Lev 24:19-20) The move to proportional retribution was a great advance over unlimited revenge. However, Jesus says, "You have heard that it was said, 'An eye for an eye and a tooth for a tooth.' But I say to you, Do not resist an evildoer. But if anyone strikes you on the right cheek, turn the other also; and if anyone wants to sue you and take your coat, give your cloak as well; and if anyone forces you to go one mile, go also the second mile." (Matt 5:38-41) As Walter Wink points out in *The Powers That Be*, Jesus always resists evil.[2] He names it and resists it. The better translation is the one found in the epistles, "Do not repay evil for evil." (Rom 12:17; 1 Thes 5:15; 1 Pet 3:9) Wink affirms the Scholars Version of this Scripture "Don't react violently against the one who is evil."

At the Last Supper, Jesus reframes and breaks the cycles of violence and retribution by saying that the naming should lead to bread, to forgiveness, and to reconciliation. In Matthew 18:21-22, Jesus takes us from the unlimited revenge of Lamech to unlimited forgiveness. "Then Peter came and said to him 'Lord, if another member of the church sins against me, how often should I forgive? As many as seven times?' Jesus said to him, "Not seven times, but, I tell you, seventy-seven times." Forgiveness is always a gift that no one can manipulate or coerce. In Matthew 18, in the parable of the unmerciful servant, Jesus makes it clear, however, that if we do not offer forgiveness, we will not be able to experience forgiveness. This is not as a result of forgiveness not being offered, but because of our inability to open our hearts to receive it. The result of the failure to forgive is the ongoing cycles of harm, retribution and violence. Bishop Tutu has written a book whose title makes this point, *No Future Without Forgiveness*. He says, ". . . because of forgiveness, there is a future."[3]

The frame within which Jesus calls us to live out our lives is not the frame of naming to punish, but the frame of naming to give bread. Here we move from blaming to naming, from punishment to accountability, from retribution to forgiveness.

The naming becomes a different reality in the context of the gift of bread and forgiveness. When the second step in the process after naming is giving bread, this changes the tone of the naming. It does not have the tone of blaming or humiliation. It does not have the "feel" of a statement to punish or wound or humiliate or dismiss.

It creates a difference in the speaker and in the hearer. It opens up a different spirit in the speaker. It opens up in the hearer, in large part because of this different spirit, the possibility of openness to real accountability as opposed to a purely defensive response. There is a judgment here, but it is the judgment of love.

The giving of bread does not negate the reality that our deeds have consequences, that accountability is important. Jesus says at the Last Supper, "For the Son of Man goes as it is written of him, but woe to that one by whom the Son of Man is betrayed! It would have been better for that one not to have been born." (Mark 14:21) We read in Matthew, that Judas recognized his sin, threw down the pieces of silver in the temple and hanged himself. (Matt 27:3-5) There are consequences for our actions. Some actions are so contrary to God's plan for life that it would have been better not to have been born. However, none of this is seen here as God's or Jesus' retribution against Judas. The hanging is self-imposed.

The naming and the giving of bread have the potential of making all things new. Was Jesus reaching out to Judas and giving him the opportunity to reconsider his plan? He was clearly reaching out to the person he called "Friend" in Gethsemane. In the garden, he said to Judas, "Friend, why are you here?" (Matt 26:50) There is in this statement a sense that Judas, after the supper, might not have betrayed Jesus. Judas was given the opportunity of a new life.

The Table of Reconciliation

What Jesus has done is transform both the way we deal with conflict, differences, and harm as well as the way we experience Holy Communion.

Remembering Jesus' Last Supper as we participate in today's ritual of Holy Communion, we see the Table as a place where we receive the gift of communal as well as personal forgiveness. We are also called to forgive. We see the Table as the place where we receive the word of reconciliation but also where we are spiritually formed into reconcilers, empowered to name and give bread, empowered to practice reconciliation. As Paul says, "everything has become new! All this is from God, who reconciled us to himself through Christ, and has given us the ministry of reconciliation: that is, in Christ God was reconciling the world to himself, not counting their trespasses against them, and entrusting the message of reconciliation to us." (2 Cor 5:17-19)

What might it look like if we truly remembered and deeply internalized the lessons of the Last Supper? What might this mean for our practice of Holy Communion? What might this mean for the way we live our lives together? In addition to affecting our life away from the Table, what if we could somehow find times to name our conflicts at the Table, practice the ministry of reconciliation at the Table and give bread to each other? More important, what might this mean for our world, for our cosmos, if this Table truly becomes a place of healing and reconciliation?

One of my favorite quotations is from Philo of Alexandria: "Be kind for everyone is involved in a great struggle."[4] If we could express at the Table our joys and pains, gratitude and conflicts, these words might become real to us. What might this mean for our understanding and experience of praise, confession and sharing the Word at the Table as we prepare ourselves for receiving the bread and the wine?

Another favorite quotation is from Henry Wadsworth Longfellow: "If we could read the secret history of our enemies, we should find in each [person's] life sorrow and suffering enough to disarm all hostility."[5] In those circumstances where we fail to reconcile after leaving our gifts at the altar, (Matt 5:23-24) what if we brought the person we should seek out and be reconciled with to the Table, where we could, in the presence and with the assistance of others in the community, listen to each other's stories, experience each others joys and sorrows and pursue the journey of reconciliation together in community?

I will conclude with a story from the South African Truth and Reconciliation Commission. In the days of *apartheid*, seven youth were killed by the South African military in an ambush. One of the men who participated in executing the youth testified before the Commission. In the room were the mothers of these young men. After he finished testifying, the mothers were asked if they wanted to say anything. The spokeswoman for the group of mothers said that they did want to speak. She turned to the young man and said, "You are going to listen to our anger. Sit there and listen." One after another, these mothers spoke of the pain they had suffered. Then, after all had finished talking, one of the mothers turned to the man, who was totally crushed, and said, "Come here. Come here; let me hold you. Let me forgive you. I have no son, now. But I want you to be my son, so that you will never do these things again." She named the conflict.   She then offered bread—indeed, her life. Thanks be to God.

Reflection Questions

1. What are some of your experiences where naming led to retribution?

2. Describe your experiences where not naming the conflict created dis-ease, and naming it moved it to a better place.

3. What are lessons you have learned about how to name the conflict in a way that opens up a conversation, instead of closing it down?

4. How does Jesus' action of naming in order to give bread reframe your understanding of reality, including how to deal with conflict?

5. Where have you experienced the gift of bread in the midst of conflict?

Notes

1. Reinhold Niebuhr, *The Nature and Destiny of Man, Volume 1. Human Nature* (New York: Charles Scribner's Sons, 1941), 182.

2. Walter Wink, *The Powers That Be* (New York: Doubleday, 1998), 99-101.

3. Desmond Tutu, *No Future Without Forgiveness* (New York: Doubleday, 1999).

4. www.entwagon.com/cgi-bin/quotes/author.pl?auth=Philo

5. www.quotedb.com/quotes/1825

Chapter Two

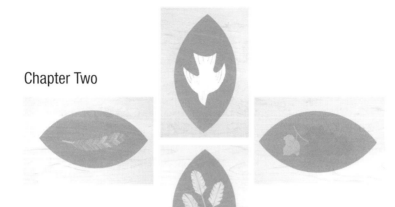

Holy Communion in the Life of the Church
The Theology and Experience of Reconciliation

GAYLE CARLTON FELTON

> *Consider the Lord's Supper, secondly, as a mercy from God to man.*
> *As God, whose mercy is over all his works, and particularly over the*
> *children of men, knew there was but one way for man to be happy*
> *like himself, namely, by being like him in holiness; as he knew we*
> *could do nothing toward this of ourselves, he has given us certain*
> *means of obtaining his help. One of these is the Lord's Supper,*
> *which of his infinite mercy he hath given for this very end: that*
> *through this means we may be assisted to attain those blessings*
> *which he hath prepared for us; that we may obtain holiness on*
> *earth and everlasting glory in heaven.*[1]

> *Meeting with the risen Lord at the heart of worship must never be*
> *a dead end! It is a turnabout, a transformation point for the out-*
> *ward journey into a needy and hurting world. Home is not only*
> *where you go for rest, belonging, and nourishment; it is where iden-*
> *tity and mission are formed and from which we go to serve.*[2]

The Christian church was born in conflict. Jesus, an observant Jew, practiced the Law in ways that the political and religious leaders of his day judged to be offensive. For this, Jesus was arrested, charged, condemned to death, and crucified. But, God's verdict was resurrection. God raised to life the one who had been condemned and made him, according to the Easter message, Lord of all. The early narratives tell us that the "beloved community" of those who had known and followed Jesus recognized that the conflict was not over. Jesus was Lord, but this faith claim was contested at every turn. Yet the beloved community persisted, "devoted to the apostles' teaching and fellowship, to the breaking of bread and the prayers." (Acts 2:42) Those who had eaten and drunk with Jesus during his lifetime and after his resurrection were living reminders to the world of the Lord it did not yet recognize. The risen Christ lived in them as Lord over all that was not yet in Christ, all that was contending with other loyalties, all that was driven by fear. The startling gift is that we who live in the twenty-first century are included in this eating and drinking with our Lord. We too experience Jesus at the table. We too are to be witnesses to what we experience.

Eucharist and Witness

The experience of eating and drinking with him after he rose from the dead is central to the contemporary church, as it is to the church in all ages and places. A close connection exists between the meal and the way Christians live out our relationships, even and especially in relationships of conflict and alienation. We often treat Holy Communion as if it were an other-worldly moment disconnected from the rest of life. The Scriptures and the ritual for Holy Communion make it clear that those who eat and drink with Jesus are witnesses in all of life—even where there is tension, exclusion, anger, and hurt. We bear witness that all of our conflict, both in the church and in the larger arenas of human struggle, is canopied by the compassionate and forgiving Lord. As witnesses we embody this message that pardons guilt and overcomes the power of sin. We who eat and drink with him on this side of the Easter experience are witnesses of reconciliation. We know the way of reconciliation, even when we are participants in conflict.

This chapter affirms the foundational understanding of the centrality of Holy Communion in the life of the beloved community. The Eucharist is our lifeline—our connection to the one through whom "we offer ourselves in praise and thanksgiving as a holy and living sacrifice."[3] Historically and in the present day, the sacrament functions as context and empowerment for reconciliation within and beyond the beloved community.

Current Teachings and Understandings of Eucharist

The twentieth-century Christian community took a surprisingly fresh look at the significance of the sacraments in the life of the church. Encouraged by the work of the Second Vatican Council and the publication of *Baptism, Eucharist and Ministry* by the World Council of Churches, United Methodism participated in sacramental recovery. Our General Conference in 1996 approved *By Water and the Spirit: A United Methodist Understanding of Baptism*. In 2004 the General Conference adopted *This Holy Mystery: A United Methodist Understanding of Holy Communion* (henceforth referred to as *THM*). Both documents were declared "official interpretive statement[s] of theology and practice in The United Methodist Church."[4]

From the Catholic and Protestant reassessment comes the realization that life around the Eucharistic table is central to Christian practice and experience. It is no longer an appendix tacked on to the service of proclamation of the word. Most Christian churches now have adopted liturgical rites for the Lord's Day that include "Word **and** Table." Even when the service does not include Holy Communion, the shape of the liturgy remains "Word and Table." *THM* holds the vision of weekly Eucharist as normative:

> Congregations of The United Methodist Church are encouraged to move toward a richer sacramental life, including weekly celebration of the Lord's Supper at the services on the Lord's Day, as advocated by the general orders of Sunday worship in *The United Methodist Hymnal* and *The United Methodist Book of Worship*.[5]

If we truly believe that nourishment and strength for our spiritual journeys come to us through Holy Communion, weekly celebration will be seen as minimal. Perhaps we may even affirm Charles Wesley's prayer to "Restore the daily sacrifice."[6]

Grace and the Means of Grace

One of the purposes of Part One of *THM* is to set our understanding of Eucharist within Wesleyan theology in general and especially within the Wesleyan way of salvation. John Wesley insisted that all persons stand in need of God's saving grace and that all who are willing can receive it. According to *THM*, "Grace is God's love toward us, God's free and undeserved gift."[7] Grace works in our lives in many ways, according to our needs. Grace is always prevenient and is experienced as convicting, justifying, sanctifying, and perfecting. Before we can even consider reconciliation of any other kind, we must first be reconciled to God. This happens when God forgives our sins, restores us to right relationship with God, and begins the process of transforming us into holiness. "While divine grace reaches us any time and in any way that God chooses, God has designated certain means or channels through which divine grace is most surely and immediately available".[8] Wesley insisted that those who seek God do so through use of the means of grace such as public worship, private and family prayer, Bible reading, fasting, and Christian conferencing. The sacraments may best be understood as especially potent means of grace, which "both express and convey the gracious love of God."[9] Sacraments are sources of the grace without which reconciliation and forgiveness and peace are impossible.

The grace received through Eucharist nourishes and sustains us on the journey of Christian life. Wesley wrote, "This is the food of our souls: This gives strength to perform our duty, and leads us on to perfection."[10] Holy Communion offers us the healing and wholeness that are fundamental to the cessation of conflict, internal and external. *The United Methodist Book of Worship* explains:

> Spiritual healing is God's work of offering persons balance, harmony, and wholeness of body, mind, spirit, and relationships through confession, forgiveness, and reconciliation. Through such healing God works to bring about reconciliation between God and humanity, among individuals and communities, within each person, and between humanity and the rest of creation.[11]

According to 2 Corinthians 5:17-21, the work of Christ was to reconcile us to God. Christ has now committed to us the continuation of that ministry of reconciliation with every person. "The grace we receive at the Lord's Table enables us to perform our ministry and mission, to continue his work in the world—the work of redemption, reconciliation, peace, and justice. As we commune we become aware of the worth and needs of other people and are reminded of our responsibility. . . . Remembering the revolutionary Jesus, we are impelled to challenge unjust practices and systems that perpetuate political, economic, and social inequity and discrimination."[12] The healing of conflict is not attained through ignoring violence and injustice or by refusing to engage them. Authentic reconciliation demands change in personal and systemic practices. To engage in righteous conflict is our inescapable duty.

The Presence of Christ

United Methodists affirm the real presence of Christ in the sacrament of the Lord's Supper. This affirmation places us within the historic catholic tradition of Christianity and in accord with the teaching of John and Charles Wesley. *THM* explicitly states that Christ is present and that "Through Jesus Christ and in the power of the Holy Spirit, God meets us at the table."[13] While we agree on the importance of "remembering" Christ and his life, death, and resurrection, we seek to move beyond the "memorialist" view that is dominant in many congregations. We are not simply recalling something that Christ did for us 2,000 years ago, but also experiencing what Christ is doing here and now in the sacrament itself. "The divine presence is a living reality and can be experienced by participants; it is not a remembrance of the Last Supper and the Crucifixion only."[14] The teaching of the real presence is more than a doctrinal correction. It is the imaginative, fertile soil in which the seed of expectancy can be planted in hope of encountering the risen Christ. The one proclaimed in the service of the word is the one we meet at the table. All the fullness of Christ, "the exact imprint of God's very being" (Heb 1:3), is present to us. As we partake of the sacrament, Christ nourishes the church and takes us into the divine life and character. So nourished and transformed, we go out into the world to work for reconciliation and peace.

Christ's Invitation

"Holy Communion always offers grace."[15] As in baptism, grace is faithfully offered and made available, but this gracious initiative must be followed by a willing acceptance on the part of those who hunger to meet Christ. Affirmation of the real presence is the basis of the invitation to commune.

> The invitation to the Table comes from the risen and present Christ. Christ invites to his Table those who love him, repent of sin, and seek to live as Christian disciples. Holy Communion is a gift of God to the church and an act of the community of faith. By responding to this invitation we affirm and deepen our personal relationship with God through Jesus Christ and our commitment to membership and mission in the body of Christ.[16]

Clearly this invitation is more than a summons to come and share a warm, fuzzy feeling. The invitation calls us to an alternative way of being in the world.

This alternative way of being in the world is unconditional from God's side. We glory in this unconditional love of God. However, as those who share in the fear, brokenness, and devastation of the dominant culture, we need conscious and willing repentance. Christ's invitation requires of us a "No" to sin and death, as is pledged in baptism, so that we may say an unqualified "Yes" to the mercy and mystery of love made known to us at the Table.

Christ invites us to come and share in an alternative to the anxiety and fear we experience and enact daily. It is as if Christ is saying to us, "Come to the Table of perfect love that casts out all fear and anxiety. Here is more than enough! All the fullness of God is here. When you come to this Table, greed motivated by fear will forever be inappropriate and unnecessary. Repent of it. When you come to this Table, all exclusion, hate, and vengeance must be left in God's keeping. Come now; come, and count on God's generosity toward all." This invitation includes confession and pardon. The invitation requires the gathered community to deal with its own brokenness and sin. Love shared, not sin remaining, is the focus of the Eucharistic meal. The meal is for those who have forsaken conflict. The invitation, confession, and pardon call us to anticipate the new heaven and new earth.

The Holy Communion Elements as Expressions and Vehicles of Reconciliation

The elements of bread and wine are both expressions and vehicles of the divine grace through which forgiveness and reconciliation come. It is of enormous significance that, on the last night of his earthly life, Jesus chose to use bread and wine to communicate to his disciples. The bread and wine were the ordinary constituents of a meal. Jesus did not make them into something different; he used them as they were—just as Christ uses us. Bread and wine are products of the natural world of God's creation; they bespeak the goodness and abundance of nature provided for human enjoyment. Bread and wine are also products of human effort; they bespeak the proper use of God's creation to nourish and enrich human life. The bread and wine exemplify the divine intention that human beings use, enjoy, protect, and share the natural environment. The conflict that wracks our world includes our alienation from the created order. One aspect of the reconciliation that we so badly need is the healing of our alienation from God's natural world.

In the Old and New Testaments, bread represents God's sustenance of humanity and the significance of our eating together. During his ministry Jesus shared bread with his followers and with his opponents. In John 6, Jesus used the imagery of bread to signify his nature and mission. The single loaf of Eucharistic bread symbolizes unity in the midst of a fractured world. The loaf represents God's intention for the world and for the church. In the words of William McElvaney, "The common loaf evokes the hidden reality that we are a single fabric of hurting and hoping humanity."[17] When we look at the single loaf we are reminded of our personal need for wholeness. We recognize that reconciliation on any other level depends upon our reconciliation to God through Christ—our own restoration to right relationship with the divine.

When the loaf is broken and shared, it becomes a vehicle through which divine grace is made available to us. We are shown that all authentic love and mercy come from one source and that we receive in order to give. No one is excluded from the Table of the Lord. All may come to receive bread; all are in need of grace. At this Table all human distinctions vanish. There is neither righteous nor unrighteous, rich nor poor, black nor white, Asian nor Latino, male nor female, gay nor straight. Conflict will never cease until we realize that God has no interest in our assignments of status and judgments of value. God's love is all-inclusive. In the very act of sharing with all, the Eucharist confronts our sin of making distinctions and holding onto divisions rooted in fear and self-centeredness.

The single chalice or cup of wine similarly expresses the hope for oneness. The wine (or juice) is the sign of the covenant relationship between God and God's people. In the history of ancient Israel, God used blood to mark the ratification of covenants. When Jesus lifted the cup in the upper room, he spoke of the wine as the new covenant in his blood. While God's covenant with the Jewish people was neither abolished nor superceded, Jesus established a new covenant, in accord with the word of some of the prophets (Jer 31:31-34). The wine in the common cup represents for us the covenant between Christ and the church, established through the life, death, and resurrection of Christ. When we drink, we reaffirm our place in the covenant community that we entered through baptism. This covenant is the basis of our hope for reconciliation and peace with justice. God has come to us in Christ and overcome the effects of sin. God offers new life in Christ. In this new life we find the empowerment to work for renewed relationships in every arena of human existence.

Shaping a Community for Reconciliation

One of the functions of Holy Communion is its role in forming the gathered Christian congregation into a community of evangelism inspired and empowered to reach out to the world. This imperative is well-expressed in *The United Methodist Discipline 2004*, ¶ 128:

> The people of God, who are the church made visible in the world, must convince the world of the reality of the gospel or leave it unconvinced. There can be no evasion or delegation of this responsibility; the church is either faithful as a witnessing and serving community, or it loses its vitality and its impact on an unbelieving world.

Outreach !! [handwritten margin note]

If the church is to be the instrument of healing and peace in the world, its people must be shaped for this ministry through the grace made available in the Eucharist:

> Claim me for Thy service, claim
> All I have and all I am.
> Take my soul and body's powers,
> Take my memory, mind, and will,
> All my goods, and all my hours,
> All I know, and all I feel,
> All I think, and speak, and do;
> Take my heart—but make it new.[18]

Good prayer [handwritten margin note]

As channels of reconciliation and justice, we must be molded in the image of the risen Christ made known to us in the breaking of the bread. This is expressed in the rituals:

> Pour out your Holy Spirit on us gathered here, and on these gifts of bread and wine. Make them be for us the body and blood of Christ, that we may be for the world the body of Christ, redeemed by his blood.[19]

The Holy Spirit working through the sacrament makes the elements, to us who commune, vehicles of the transforming grace of God in Christ. So transformed, we become vehicles of that same grace; we are enabled to live in sacramental ways. Shaped by sacrament into sacrament, the church becomes the divine instrument through which the world can be transformed. Recognition of this responsibility is voiced in the prayer after receiving:

> Eternal God, we give you thanks for this holy mystery in which you have given yourself to us. Grant that we may go into the world in the strength of your Spirit, to give ourselves for others, in the name of Jesus Christ our Lord.[20]

During his earthly life Jesus went out of his way to eat with all kinds of people—his followers, his enemies, and those who were marginalized in his society. Ignoring the criticism of his choice of meal companions, Jesus enjoyed table fellowship, taught, and witnessed to God's inclusive love. The phrase in our ritual which Christians should perhaps find most comforting and most challenging is the simple statement that he "ate with sinners." Thank God that he did, and that he does. Pray that we might exemplify such love.

One of the most faithful things that Christians can do as we participate in the Lord's Supper is consciously to observe and reflect upon those who are absent from the Table. Are there those who feel shunned or unworthy? Are whole ethnic groups missing or scarcely represented? Are all socio-economic and educational classes included? Are children, the elderly, the infirm present? Are there persons with physical, emotional, and mental incapacities? Are there persons of diverse sexual orientations and identities? Where are the poor, the homeless, the destitute? What about those confined to penal and custodial institutions? Who else among God's beloved people are absent? If the community gathered around the Table of the Lord does not reflect the variety and inclusiveness of all God's people, the church is defying the Christ who ordered: "Go out at once into the streets and lanes of the town and bring in the poor, the crippled, the blind, and the lame . . . . Go out into the roads and lanes, and compel people to come in, so that my house may be filled" (Luke 14:21, 23).

The grace of the Lord's Table is not limited to the physical space of the sanctuary. Persons who are unwillingly absent should be included in the celebration by the taking of consecrated elements to them. This includes those who are homebound or institutionalized, as well as those who have to work on Sunday. *THM* states, "The Table may be extended, in a timely manner, to include those unable to attend because of age, illness, or similar condition. Laypeople may distribute the consecrated elements in the congregation and extend them to members who are unavoidably absent."[21] In this practice the church reaches out to gather in those who are physically separated and who may become emotionally and spiritually separated as well. Even when we do not actually serve the consecrated elements, Christians have the responsibility to share Eucharistic grace. We reach out by extending ourselves in acts of friendship and compassion. We gather in the alienated through our witness of inclusion, welcome, and justice. In such actions we work toward reconciling and healing of the torn fabric of humanity.

Extending the Table Into the World

The Wesleyan revival in eighteenth-century England was spiritual, sacramental, and social. These three aspects must be held together today if the church is to be effective in its ministry of reconciliation. Spiritual revival can be kindled and sustained through the Lord's Supper; a revived church can be the instrument of healing in the society:

The grace received in the Lord's Supper is a "grace unto." It is grace unto forgiveness, new life, and sanctification. At every point of our journeys of salvation, the Eucharist offers the grace we need—to repent, to be healed and forgive, to trust, to be transformed, to be reconciled, to resist sin, to continue to grow ever more perfectly into the image of Christ, to recognize ourselves as the body of Christ in and for the world. There should be a direct linkage between our partaking of Holy Communion and our living lives of committed Christian discipleship.[22]

In the Wesleyan paradigm, justification and regeneration are followed by the lifelong process of sanctification or growth in holiness. This holiness is both personal and social. Any attempt to separate the two is unfaithful. Wesley proclaimed this linkage and lived it: "The Gospel of Christ knows no religion, but social; no holiness but social holiness."[23] As a young man in the Holy Club at Oxford, Wesley led others in "works of piety," which included visiting the horrendous English jails and ministering to prisoners. When he was eighty-one years old, Wesley wrote in his journal:

> So on this and the four following days, I walked through the town [London] and begged two hundred pounds in order to clothe them that wanted it most. But it was hard work, as most of the streets were filled with melting snow which often lay ankle deep, so that my feet were steeped in snow-water nearly from morning till evening. I held it out pretty well till Saturday evening I was laid up with a violent flux which increased every hour, till at six in the morning Dr. Whitehead called upon me.[24]

good motivation

That quality of compassion and commitment is essential if the contemporary church is to change the conditions that breed and feed conflict.

John Wesley was concerned about alleviating the suffering of the poor, the imprisoned, the sick, and others who were hurting. He also recognized that charity was not enough. If the sources of suffering were to be addressed, if reconciliation and healing were to take place in the society, systemic changes were required. Poverty, as Wesley understood it, was the result of misuse of the wealth of the community and had to be addressed by responsible use of resources. He sought to provide work for the unemployed. Slavery was totally unjustifiable on economic or other grounds; it was an affront to the God who created all persons, and had to be abolished. The liquor trade destroyed minds and bodies, misused grain which could have fed the poor, and diverted money from valid use. The criminal justice system was unjust and overly severe; Wesley campaigned for reform. He worked diligently to provide schooling for children. Not only did the Methodists open medical dispensaries, but Wesley also worked for preventive health care. While he was not a pacifist, Wesley was committed to peace: "I am persuaded love and tender measures will do far more than violence."[25] Wesley was convinced that the power of God working through Christian people expressed itself in social transformation.

Wesley identified Holy Communion as "the grand channel whereby the grace of his Holy Spirit was conveyed to the souls of all the children of God."[26] Through this divine grace conflicts can be mediated, forgiveness granted, and reconciliation actualized in our world. God is alive and active within and among us and the Eucharist is the central portal into this divine life for the Christian church.

Reflection Questions

1. How do you understand the relationship between participation in the Eucharist and Christian witness in the world?

2. How does the recovery of authentic sacramental theology and practice affect the life of your congregation?

3. What are the implications for The United Methodist Church of the open communion table? How does this change your understanding of justice?

5. Who are the absent ones at our communion tables? How can we extend the table to include all?

Notes

1. John Wesley, "The Duty of Constant Communion"

2. William K. McElvaney, *Eating and Drinking at the Welcome Table: The Holy Supper for All People* (Atlanta: Chalice Press, 1998), xiii.

3. From "A Service of Word and Table I," *The United Methodist Hymnal* (Nashville: The United Methodist Publishing House, 1989) 10.

4. *The Book of Resolutions of the United Methodist Church* (Nashville: The United Methodist Publishing House, 2004), p. 857-876, 883-931. This wording is in the petitions to General Conference for approval. Both documents are printed in *The United Methodist Book of Resolutions.* Commentary and study editions by Gayle Carlton Felton are available from Cokesbury.

5. Gayle Carlton Felton, *This Holy Mystery: A United Methodist Understanding of Holy Communion* (Nashville: Discipleship Resources, 2005), 34.

6. J. Ernest Rattenbury, *The Eucharistic Hymns of John and Charles Wesley* (Akron: The Order of Saint Luke, 1990), stanza 16 of hymn 166, H-55.

7. Felton, p. 15.

8. Ibid.

9. Ibid., 16.

10. "The Duty of Constant Communion," Sermon 101, 3.

11. *The United Methodist Book of Worship* (Nashville: The United Methodist Publishing House, 1992), 613.

12. Felton, 20.

13. Ibid., 23.

14. Ibid.

15. Ibid.

16. Ibid., 25.

17. McElvaney, 23.

18 Rattenbury, stanzas 3-4, hymn 155, H-50.

19. *The United Methodist Hymnal*, 10.

20. Ibid., 11.

21. Felton, 37.

22. Ibid., 56.

23. John Wesley, *"List of Poetical Works Published by the Rev. Messrs. John and Charles Wesley,"* in *The Works of John Wesley,* vol. XIV (Grand Rapids: Zondervan Publishing House, n.d.), 321.

24. Wesley, Journal, 4 January 1785, in *The Works of John Wesley,* vol. 23 (Nashville: Abingdon Press, 1995), 340.

25. Wesley, "Letter to Mr. Thomas Rankin," October 20, 1775, *Works,* vol. 12, 330.

26. Wesley, "Upon Our Lord's Sermon on the Mount," Sermon 26, 11, *Works,* vol. 5, 338.

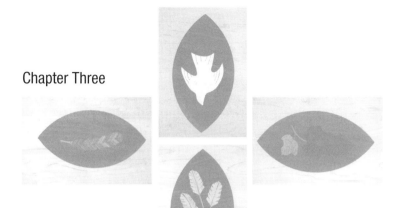

Chapter Three

Holy Communion and the Vision of the Beloved Community

LARRY M. GOODPASTER

> *"You're no longer wandering exiles. This kingdom of faith is now your home country. You're no longer strangers or outsiders. You* belong *here. . . ." (Ephesians 2:19, from* The Message *by Eugene H. Peterson)*

I grew up in a tradition that reserved the first Sunday of every month as the occasion for "having communion." We could count on it, as well as the hymns that would be sung, regardless of the season of the church year. More often than not the sacrament was tacked on at the end of the service and the ritual hurried in order to "get out on time." After I was ordained and appointed as a pastor, I began to understand the awesome responsibility of consecrating the bread and the wine and offering it as "the body of Christ for the world." For more than thirty years it has been a high and holy honor for me to preside at the Table, to say the Prayer of Great Thanksgiving, and to consecrate and serve the elements of Holy Communion. This sacred moment allows me the privilege of lifting this sign of God's grace before the gathered people. It was, and is, and I hope always will be, a humbling experience for me as a called, credentialed, and ordained person who dares to offer the sacrament.

Over the years I have also grown in recognition of and appreciation for the sacredness of the *gathering* at the Table. After I have followed the rubrics and extended the invitation, the people come to the altar or the table or the stations, depending on the setting and custom in which the elements are offered, and they come from a wide variety of circumstances and situations. The many roads their lives have taken that now converge on their way with others to the Table. As a pastor, I see people gathering from different socio-economic backgrounds, different political parties, different theological viewpoints, and with different styles of dress. In a sense what I observe each time I am part of a Service of Holy Communion is a community of people who might not otherwise eat together or even associate with one another were it not for the Table. The God who extends grace and love to the world, who was manifest in Jesus the Christ, and who is present at the Table calls us into community. It is never lost on me that I too am included in that community—thankfully!

This mysterious coming together and modeling of 'community' is the subject of this chapter. As we think about how communion and community are linked, I invite you to journey with me. We will begin with a Scripture story to provide a framework for our reflection.

A Biblical Story for Setting the Context

An intriguing story is recorded in Second Samuel. It is a David story, although perhaps not as well known as some of David's other exploits. The episode is filled with grace and hope, and offers a perspective about relationships, renewal, restoration, community, and meals.

> David asked, "Is there still anyone left of the house of Saul to whom I may show kindness for Jonathan's sake?" Now there was a servant of the house of Saul whose name was Ziba, and he was summoned to David. The king said to him, "Are you Ziba?" And he said, "At your service!" The king said, "Is there anyone remaining of the house of Saul to whom I may show the kindness of God?" Ziba said to the king, "There remains a son of Jonathan; he is crippled in his feet." (2 Sam 9:1-3)

David had promised Jonathan that he would protect and defend all of Jonathan's descendants. First Samuel 20 and 24 detail the story of these two friends sealing their friendship and the promise that Jonathan's family would forever live under David's care. Now that David has come to power and united the tribes, it is time to make good on that earlier promise. David has not forgotten the commitment he made and takes measures to find out if there is anyone left.

Now we are introduced to Jonathan's son, who is described there and in the closing verse of the chapter (as if for emphasis) as one who is *"lame in both feet."* The story behind that reality is mentioned in 2 Samuel, chapter 4. As David is rising to power and Saul is losing his, there is an on-going story of betrayal and murder, double-crossing and suspicion. One of David's leaders, Joab, murders one of Saul's leaders, Abner, who had tried to switch sides. When news of the death of Abner reaches the household of Jonathan, a nurse, in her haste to get out of the city, drops the five-year-old Mephibosheth. That is all we know, except that the chapter notes that he became lame as a result of this accident.

As our story continues, David, having promised to take care of the descendants of Jonathan, discovers that the son named Mephibosheth appears to be the last in the genealogical line. David invites him into his house. The next actions are quite amazing.

> Mephibosheth son of Jonathan son of Saul came to David, and fell on his face and did obeisance. David said, "Mephibosheth!" He answered, "I am your servant." David said to him, "Do not be afraid, for I will show you kindness for the sake of your father Jonathan; I will restore to you all the land of your grandfather Saul, and you yourself shall eat at my table always." (2 Sam 9:6-7)

In what amounts to a very generous and astounding gesture, David restores the land of Saul to this grandson. Since we are familiar with the risks of power and authority and the potential for greed and grabbing, this jubilee gift of land is to be celebrated. David did not have to do this! After all, to the victor go the spoils! However, by doing so David has not only fulfilled his earlier promise, but has gone beyond what might be expected, especially given the inheritance rules at that time. Mephibosheth and Jonathan's family are thus rescued from any financial trouble or future concerns about security.

The second surprising moment comes as David extends the offer of table fellowship and food for the remainder of Mephibosheth's life! Not only does he settle in Jerusalem with land that provides an income for him, but he becomes a constant presence at David's table. The chapter ends with an observation: *"Mephibosheth lived in Jerusalem, for he always ate at the king's table."* (2 Sam 9:13) Can you imagine the conversations that took place among those who were on the inside of David's entourage when Mephibosheth shows up for that first meal? Having presented his invitation and his identification, he is escorted to the main table, and the grumbling born of misperception and prejudice begins.

"How is it that he gets to sit there when I am over here?"

"There goes the neighborhood!"

"I thought we were through with that family."

"Well I suppose we will all have to take turns helping him to his chair, taking his crutches, helping him cut his meat, and assisting him when he is ready to leave the table."

As with all of Scripture, much depends on how we approach the reading. If we read this ninth chapter politically or from a purely historical critical method, we will see little else but palace paranoia and political savvy. Some might suggest that David is simply eliminating the competition to his throne by bringing Saul's grandson to the table and installing him in a prominent position. It becomes a convenient way for David to keep an eye on him. Or, to buy him off, if you will! But to pursue this method alone is to read in to it too much of our own experience of human history, too much of our own cynical views of power and authority. To see it through the lens of a hermeneutic of suspicion is to invite a pessimistic view of the actions.

However, if we listen from the perspective of salvation history and faith, we can experience the story in a very different way. It takes on the flavor of grace: of one who does not deserve to be at the table suddenly finding a permanent place. It is a story of a table that becomes a community, a place where everyone can gather, even those who are differently abled, who are from the wrong family, even those who are unlike anyone else sharing the bread at the table.

The World in Which We Live

We live in a frighteningly fragmented, distorted world. It is a world that is being torn apart in confusion and chaos by conflicting voices, competing ideologies, and growing economic disparities. Poverty, hunger, abuse and neglect, hatred and suspicion combine to shatter the dreams of too many people, starting with the children. Mephibosheth is all around us: crippled lives, broken dreams, isolated and marginalized people. If we make an honest assessment of our own lives, we may find that each one of us is in some way Mephibosheth.

The world in which we live is not only characterized by unhealthy and dysfunctional systems and people, but those very dysfunctions contribute to explosive situations. Martin Marty describes the world we inhabit as a place ". . . where strangers meet strangers with gunfire, barrier walls, spiritually landmined paths, the spirit of revenge, and the record of intransigence . . . ."[1] When we walk a road that is marked by vengeance and violence, when hostility is the response of choice, and when every waking moment is filled with fear and anxiety, any vision of a beloved community is clouded and elusive.

The church and the many denominational expressions of the universal church too often mirror society and the culture of this postmodern era. We draw our organizational charts as if we were like any other business or service club rather than a community of grace; we find our metaphors and image-makers in the stories of the culture that surround us rather than in the Gospel story; and, we lose our voice in reactive negativity rather than in a proactive affirmation of faith. We find ourselves far from the image of being one as Christ prayed in the seventeenth chapter of the Gospel of John, preferring instead to choose up sides: Lutherans and Episcopalians, Methodists and Baptists. Not content with the lines drawn across the streets and highways, we divide ourselves further with enough affinity groups, special interests and pieces of the whole to cause confusion, and to make unity and a community that is loved and that offers love a distant dream. We become alienated from and strangers to one another. Like Mephibosheth it feels as if someone, in a panic, dropped us and we are left to limp through life into an uncertain future. What then shall we do?

The Meal by Which We Are Shaped

"In the midst of the personal and systemic brokenness in which we live, we yearn for everlasting fellowship with Christ and ultimate fulfillment of the divine plan. Nourished by sacramental grace, we strive to be formed into the image of Christ and to be made instruments for transformation in the world."[2] Eucharist, the sacrament of Holy Communion, continues to be an experience in which people of faith and people searching for faith discover not only a ritual, not only bread and a cup, but also the transforming grace of God in a tangible way. While the many traditions of the Christian church have varied opinions on the way in which the sacrament is to be served and received, and in which Christ is present at the Table, there is a common sense that something holy, something transformational, something grace-filled happens in this sacrament. As a result, the Eucharist may indeed provide a way forward and a way for this divided, suspicious world to finds its way to a different place, an alternative and holy vision of what it means to be in community.

It is precisely at this point that the story of David and Mephibosheth has something to teach us. Our worlds have similar intrigues: fear, schism, uncertainty, political maneuvering, extremists, and terrorists. At the table David practices and extends grace, and Mephibosheth receives and experiences grace. Even with all of the possible moments of skepticism and suspicion we may encounter in this story, I sense that something holy and sacred happens, and that a relationship is born by acting on a vow taken years before. Could this become a sign of hope in a world that is broken and torn apart with hatred, war, insanity, and prejudice? Could it be that as we eat together "at the king's table" (2 Sam 9:13) we experience a grace-formed relationship that affects the way we live our lives when we leave the table? As we gather at the Table, we may discover that we will ourselves become part of the answer to the Eucharistic prayer: we really can be one in Christ, and become one with each other, and united in our mutual ministry to the world. "The grace received at the Table of the Lord can make us whole. As those who are being saved, we seek to bring healing to a broken world."[3] For Mephibosheth, being restored at the king's table meant the beginning of a new and different life, above and beyond anything he had known, or that he might have expected.

It is a sad commentary on our understanding of the Sacrament of Holy Communion that for many churches the announcement of a Sunday to celebrate the sacrament results in poor attendance. *This Holy Mystery* was the result of several years of study, reflection, and writing. The call for such a study grew out of a sense of United Methodists needing to dig deeper into the meaning and celebration of the sacraments, and needing a comprehensive theological statement about Holy Communion. The challenge remains for lay and clergy leaders to digest the implications of that study. The challenge remains to experience the healing, transforming grace that is made visible and made available to all who would come to the Table. A study document is one thing; a vibrant sacramental life that shapes and forms us as believers and followers of Jesus the Christ is something else.

In his sermon "The Duty of Constant Communion" John Wesley addresses not only the importance of celebrating the sacrament often, but also the essence of what happens at the Table. He writes that we should come for the sacrament as often as we can ". . . because the benefits of doing it are so great to all that do it in obedience to him; viz., the forgiveness of our past sins, the present strengthening and refreshing of our souls."[4] Wesley adds that ". . . through this means we may be assisted to attain those blessings which he hath prepared for us; that we may obtain holiness on earth, and everlasting glory in heaven."[5] Following Wesley's reasoning then, as we come to the Table to partake of the sacrament, and to taste and see the goodness of God, our lives can be transformed. As those who are marked for and are going on to perfection, the sacrament becomes a means of experiencing God's love and grace, and a means of going forth to live holy lives. In Wesley's account, holy lives and holy living, and moving on toward Christian perfection are nothing less than loving God with everything we are and have, and loving our neighbors with the same love we have for God and for ourselves.[6]

This holy meal is an invitation to be shaped and formed by the Christ who serves as the host. It is to participate by the power of the Spirit in the life, death, and resurrection of Jesus. Like Mephibosheth, we are invited to always be at the Table, and like him, none of us deserve to be there. It is only by the kindness of David that Mephibosheth is sitting at the table. It is only by the grace, mercy, and loving-kindness of God that we are included at the Table. But we cannot come to the Table without being affected. Mephibosheth certainly was. Those who were watching him eat David's food with them certainly were. All of those who were the beneficiaries of the table fellowship of Jesus were affected. Some were infuriated. Others were blessed. All were shaped.

Our gathering at the Table on a regular basis to partake of this holy meal may be an important link in healing the brokenness of this world and of our churches. It is at the Table that we are exposed to the Gospel story and go forth to follow the one who bids us take up a cross and walk with him. The stories of Jesus reclining in table fellowship show him eating with people from all levels of society, those on the inside and those on the outside, those who were in need of healing and knew it, and those who were in need of healing and thought they were well. We do not find him anywhere in the recorded gospel accounts eating by himself, or eating fast food or take out. There was something about being at the table that encouraged conversation, that offered grace, and that blessed the participants. In those moments, the agenda and the vision of a different life and a different world were modeled for those with eyes to see, ears to hear, and hearts to comprehend.

N. T. Wright suggests that what Jesus does in his life and teaching is to offer an alternative vision for the way we are to live, relate, and work in this world. The agenda Jesus offers is a vision of God's kingdom that is radically different from any

good #

Interesting !!

vision or agenda that might be proposed or composed by human thought and reason. Wright goes on to suggest that it is at the Table that this vision gets played out.

> "Wherever Jesus went, there seemed to be a celebration; the tradition of festive meals at which Jesus welcomed all and sundry is one of the most securely established features of almost all recent scholarly portraits. And the reason why some of Jesus' contemporaries found this so offensive is not far to seek (though not always understood). It was not just that he as an individual was associating with disreputable people; that would not have been a great offense. It was because he was doing so as a prophet of the kingdom and was indeed making these meals and their free-for-all welcome a central feature of his program. The meals spoke powerfully about Jesus' vision of the kingdom; what they said was subversive of other kingdom-agendas. Jesus' welcome symbolized God's radical acceptance and forgiveness. . . ."[7]

The Community for Which We Dream

Mephibosheth "always ate at the king's table." Not only does David move Jonathan's son to Jerusalem, not only does he restore the proceeds from the land that was originally in the family, but David expands his table to include this young man as part of a larger community. When we assemble as believers, what better picture can we paint than to be at the Table together? "As followers of Jesus, who ate with sinners and reached out to the marginalized, the church must intentionally concern itself about those who are absent from Christ's Table—those who feel unworthy, the poor, the unconverted, victims of prejudice, and others who are oppressed or neglected."[8]

Seeing the Eucharist as a community-making table invites us to faithfully and prayerfully consider who is on our guest list, a guest list that intentionally includes the Mephibosheths of our neighborhoods. Jesus demonstrates how the lessons of inclusion are to be applied in his actions. We are also invited to faithfully and prayerfully remember who serves as host and what is on the table: the body and blood of Christ, the sign of God's sacrificial love poured out for each person and for the world. This must become a both/and experience: both who is at the table and who is the host; both God's love for the world and our love in response; both God's gracious action and our faithful response. Within this context, when we begin to see everyone who is at the table with us as loved children, people of sacred worth, persons for whom Christ offered himself, we will catch a glimpse of what holds us together, not what tears us apart.

The Council of Bishops of The United Methodist Church adopted as a third phase in its initiative and emphasis on children and poverty an invitation to focus on the beloved community as our shared dream. That brief statement includes several references and descriptions of what that community will look like, and encourages all of us to dream of a different way of being the church in the world.

"In the Beloved Community, young and old, and all in between, know themselves to be formed and empowered to love others by the grace of God in Jesus Christ."

"The Beloved Community is to be a visible sign of the body of Christ in the world."

"The Beloved Community becomes reality when love of God and faith in Christ are expressed in selfless love for all the peoples of the world. This requires a complete turning away from easy religiosity."

"The Beloved Community is a dramatic sign of the presence in the world of the spirit of Jesus Christ, in which the walls of separation are broken down so that all— Jew and Gentile, male and female, young and old, slave and free, rich and poor, those near and those far away—may be one."[9]

Since moving to Montgomery, Alabama, I have often found myself in the downtown area. On almost every one of those visits, my route has taken me past the Dexter Avenue King Memorial Baptist Church, the pulpit from which Dr. Martin Luther King, Jr. caught, preached, and planted a vision that changed society. It was in Montgomery that the image of beloved community emerged in his preaching and leading. I read and remember the words of Dr. King as a prophet to this country, a voice for God's beloved community, one who glimpsed the kingdom come.

When we gather at the Table we are invited to partake of God's grace in a way that allows us to glimpse a community grounded in God, shaped by Christ, and empowered by the Spirit. What Dr. King proclaimed is that any attempt at creating such a community is possible only as we fully grasp—and are grasped by—the love of God made visible in Jesus and made victorious through the Cross. It is a community because we are made one with Christ and one with each other. It is beloved because we are loved and graced by God. It is a vision of a beloved community that is filled with images of peace and harmony, of truth and justice, of reconciliation and transformation, and of hope and trust. At the Table we are confronted with the signs, symbols, and remembrance of the Christ whose life and teachings, and whose death and resurrection held out such a vision. From the table we are sent forth to be the signs and symbols of that new community where we are, as the Eucharistic prayer phrases it, "one with Christ, one with each other, and one in ministry to all the world."

We continue to envision such a community because it has not yet fully appeared. However, the church is called upon to keep that vision alive and fresh, and to point the way to where such a community might emerge in this complex world. Gathering at the Table invites us both into remembering (calling to mind, rehearsing, and re-presenting) the sacrifice of Christ and into being re-membered (put back together, reshaped into a new creation). Gathering at the Table is also a bold affirmation of faith and a sign of what a beloved community might finally come to look like. It is "eating at the king's table" where we experience the kindness and mercy of God, as Mephibosheth discovered at David's table. What transforms our gathering and our eating is the presence of the risen Christ.

Reflection Questions

1. Recall a time when you experienced Eucharist as a transforming moment in your life. Close your eyes and contemplate that moment. What do you see and hear? By whatever means is comfortable and acceptable for you, record or share that experience.

2. How might our gathering around the Table provide a means of healing for our own lives and for our relationships? How might we then become agents of reconciliation, healing, restoration and wholeness?

3. Who are the "Mephibosheths" in your church and community today? Who is excluded? Who needs to be included? How will you open the table in your church and community to those persons?

4. What word-pictures would you employ to describe the "beloved community?" Where have you actually seen it come to life? What have you observed as obstacles to dwelling in such a community? How will you address these obstacles? Who will you invite to the Table?

Notes

1. Martin Marty, *When Faiths Collide* (Malden: Blackwell Publishing, 2005), 128.
2. Gayle Carlton Felton, *This Holy Mystery* (Nashville: Discipleship Resources, 2005), 18.
3. Ibid., 20.
4. *The Works of John Wesley* (Third Edition), volume 7 (Grand Rapids: Baker Books, 2002), 148.
5. Ibid., 150.
6. Cf., the "Great Commandment" in Matthew 22:34-40, Mark 12:28-34, and Luke 10:25-28.
7. N. T. Wright, *The Challenge of Jesus* (Downers Grove: InterVarsity Press, 1999), page 45.

8. Felton, 56.

9. Each one of the quotations listed is taken from the document "Our Shared Dream: The Beloved Community" of The Council of Bishops of The United Methodist Church (Nashville: The United Methodist Publishing House, 2003).

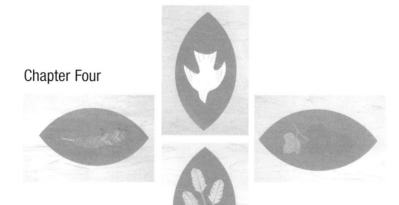

Chapter Four

Communion and Forgiveness
Awakening to the Circle of Love

MARJORIE THOMPSON

> *Communion is the word that responds to the deepest yearnings of the human heart. We are created for communion. I don't believe it is an exaggeration to say that what all people share is a life-long search for communion.*[1]

When Henri Nouwen wrote these words, he articulated more than an astute observation of the human condition. His words imply a central spiritual fact: If we are created for communion it is because communion represents the mysterious truth of the entire cosmos. Everything that exists owes its being to a vast all-encompassing circle of love. The circle of love is a metaphor for God, but our notions of its boundaries cannot be contained by a finite symbol. The immense mystery of the metaphor is captured in a saying attributed to the Christian mystic, Meister Eckhart, "God is the circle whose center is everywhere and whose circumference is nowhere."[2]

We catch our clearest vision of this circle in the incarnate Word, Jesus Christ, "the image of the invisible God." Paul writes to the Colossians that "in him all things in heaven and on earth were created, things visible and invisible . . . all things have been created through him and for him . . . and in him all things hold together." (1:15-17) From the unfathomable unity of the inner life of the Trinity, a marvelous creation comes to light, reflecting the co-inherence of divine love. In this creation all things are held together in a wonderfully dynamic web of unity, glistening with the glory of original love.

Communion, then, is the beginning and the end of all life but especially of human life created to reflect the divine image. So it should not surprise us that forgiveness—something needed only because we have damaged the original gift of unity—can only begin in communion and return to it.

My intention in this chapter is to explore three connecting themes: 1) forgiveness is rooted in communion; 2) communion makes forgiveness possible; and 3) forgiveness makes communion possible. A simpler way to put it is this: It all begins with God's love; it all ends in God's love; and only God's costly love can get us there.

Forgiveness is Rooted in Communion

Forgiveness is a ticklish subject. To some it seems an exercise in sentimental piety. To others it appears a practical or emotional impossibility within the "real world." Yet to Christians and others of good faith, it is the most powerful path to healing and redemption of which we can conceive. Even from such faith perspective, however, forgiveness is a complex matter.

It is helpful to clarify what forgiveness is not, as we tend to confuse it with other human dynamics. For example, forgiveness does not mean denying our hurt or suppressing our pain. It is not resignation to the role of victim, or making oneself submissive bait for bullies. Forgiveness does not mean putting someone "on probation" while waiting impatiently for changed behavior. Emphatically it does not mean excusing or condoning destructive behaviors. Forgiveness is not a commodity we can "purchase" through sufficiently fervent demonstrations of penitence. Nor is it merely a feeling, as it involves an entire disposition of mind, heart, and will. Finally, forgiving is not necessarily forgetting although we can learn to recall the hurt in a different light.

What, then, *is* forgiveness? Here are a few descriptions worth pondering:

> To forgive is to release oneself from the corrosive bondage of continuing anger, bitterness, and resentment.

> To forgive is to make a conscious choice to release the person who has wounded us from the sentence of our condemnation, however justified it may seem.

> Forgiveness is taking responsibility from my side to release the offender from the alienating effect of the offence on our relationship.

> To forgive is to give up the exhilaration of one's own unassailable rightness.[3]

Our efforts to forgive those who wound us are notoriously fragile and incomplete. Even for small offences, our emotional response can become so consuming that we don't know how to extricate ourselves from resentment or a thirst to retaliate. We need to start with God if we are to make progress in this practice. Forgiveness originates with God.

When we begin with God, we see that forgiving others is not our first task. The first order of business is to receive God's forgiveness. Right away this puts things in a different light. The focus shifts from the sins of others against us to our sins against God and others. Reminding us of our own role in the pervasive morass of human sin is the purpose of confession in common worship. In one of the great prayers of the tradition, we confess that "we have not loved you with our whole heart . . . we have not loved our neighbors . . . ." The failure of love is a failure to grasp our essential unity within the human family.

Every time we recite the Lord's Prayer together, we have opportunity to remember that where forgiveness is concerned, "the measure you give will be the measure you get back." (Luke 6:38) Archbishop Anthony Bloom tells the story of a French general, Maurice d'Elbee, during the revolutionary wars in France. His men had captured some of the enemy and wanted to shoot them. The general reluctantly agreed, but insisted that they should first recite the Lord's Prayer aloud. This they did. When they came to the words, "Forgive us our trespasses as we forgive those who trespass against us," they suddenly understood their situation and, weeping, let their prisoners go free.[4]

What those men understood in that moment was their common humanity with the enemy soldiers. They were in this war together as fellow sinners, and they shared the human possibility of redemption by God's grace. Through the Lord's Prayer they glimpsed what Nouwen calls "the deeper communion that already exists below the stormy waves of our restless days;" through forgiveness they took part in "the great work of love among the fellowship of the weak that is the human family."[5]

The eminent Quaker teacher Douglas Steere offers an image for this deeper communion when he writes that our souls "are interconnected in God, as though the many wicks of our lamps draw their oil from the same full cruse in which they are all immersed."[6] We are united by virtue of our creation as human beings made in the same divine image. We are also, sorrowfully, united by our common brokenness and sin. One pastoral counselor suggests that forgiveness is less something we *do* than something we *discover*: "that I am more like those who have hurt me than different from them."[7] Author Kathleen Fischer illustrates this common dynamic from her own life:

> I may be angry with a family member for criticizing me, keeping secrets, or failing to pull equal weight on family projects. Then, to my chagrin, I catch myself doing the very same thing. The illusion that others are sinful and I am perfect burst like a balloon, giving way to the realization that every one of us stands in need of mercy. No exceptions. [8]

Yet we often have difficulty perceiving this essential unity, and frequently stumble over emotional blocks to forgiveness. What will help us travel forward toward healing, reconciliation, and redemption? The hidden wholeness of our unity may be spiritual fact, but it often remains distant reality in terms of our daily, lived experience.

Forgiveness is Made Possible by Communion

We grow slowly into the habits of mind, heart, and hand that make us more forgiving persons. This is part of the life-long process of spiritual maturation called *sanctification*. Sanctification is growth in holiness of heart and life, emerging over time from our cooperation with the gracious work of the Holy Spirit. God is remarkably patient, and understands better than we the deep patterns of our resistance to love.

When we are deeply wounded or afraid, much healing and assurance of safety is required to get us past our defenses. Indeed, until we feel profoundly assured of safety and love, efforts to remove our defenses would be unwise and possibly destructive. For example, experiences of individual abuse and corporate oppression should not be forgiven prematurely. Time is needed for those who are deeply wounded to remove themselves from the abusive or oppressive circumstances if possible, or if not, to find an inwardly secure sanctuary from which to gain freedom to act in new ways. Time is required to heal, strengthen, and find ground on which to stand with dignity and self-respect. Only then will the choice to forgive have power to free the abused from "victim" status.

The most profound way we come to experience an assurance of ultimate safety is to know our beloved-ness in God's heart. This is a knowledge we can only receive as a gift; it becomes ours as we allow ourselves to possess it. But the message is there for us in Scripture if we have ears to hear. One of Henri Nouwen's greatest legacies to the church universal was to highlight this core spiritual truth: we are God's beloved children, sons and daughters of the Most High, forever embraced by a love that will not let us go. We are, both in and beyond this world, held secure in hands of utmost compassion and mercy. God's love for us is original, preceding our experience of being wounded by the imperfect love of parents, siblings, teachers, friends or colleagues. It is this "first love" from which we were fashioned, and from which we are in turn enabled to love others.

"The experience of being called the Beloved is the experience of communion," writes Nouwen. He points out that *communion* literally means *union with*. "The word *union* speaks against alienation, separation, division, conflict, competition, rivalry," evoking instead "relationship, intimacy, and mutuality."[9] Every form of love—in marriage, friendship, or spiritual devotion—is an expression of communion. To know ourselves deeply loved is to enter the realm of communion God has always intended for us.

But we often do not know our beloved-ness, to God or to others. We have internalized countless messages of self-rejection and criticism. Depending on our circumstances, we suffer a variety of negative self-images: ugly, untalented, slow, inadequate, indecisive, unlucky, impatient, or inauthentic. Even under the surface of reasonably successful lives we can feel like frauds trying somehow to appear acceptable. There may well be solid evidence of these shortcomings in our lives. But no weakness completely defines us or anyone else. We have a deeper identity, whose beauty and glory seem too good to be true: we are God's beloved. We were made from the goodness of an eternally loving heart to belong to the vast circle of divine love—made for communion. Only our refusal to receive the grace of this love can keep us from being restored to it.

The church, as the body of Christ, is the community where we discover our true identity and learn to live it more fully. It is the repository of scriptural wisdom and interpretation; the place where sacramental celebration reminds us of our true identity in Baptism and the gift of saving mercy in Holy Communion; the community where we are enjoined to live together in love as Christ loved us, learning how to work out our differences in the mind of Christ and the spirit of peace. Here we discover our need for repentance—turning away from the dynamics of death toward God's gift of life. Here we are given opportunity to receive forgiveness and to practice the art of offering it. The restoration of God's intended communion can only come about through forgiveness gratefully received and freely offered.

The sacrament we call Holy Communion is particularly instructive and powerful in relation to forgiveness. If we allow it to, its liturgy will slowly pattern us in the long journey of sanctification. One of the best ways of learning to forgive is to come often to the table where we remember God's unfathomable grace towards us in Jesus Christ. Here we experience the cross at the very center of the eternal circle of love. Its arms are spread in forgiving embrace, rejoining us as God's beloved family in joyful communion. And so, Holy Communion becomes a means of forgiveness and reconciliation—first God's toward us, and ours, in turn, towards one another.

The Lord's Supper is intimately bound up with divine forgiveness, and therefore with communion. Here is the pattern we repeat at each sacred meal.

1. The Eucharistic liturgy begins with the Great Thanksgiving, praising God for creating heaven and earth and for making us in the divine image. Here we are thanking God for the beauty, order, and unity of life, acknowledging its intended purpose of communion.

2. We admit that we have "turned away and our love failed." Sin mars the original harmony of creation, subjecting all to division, animosity, and death. We have—individually and collectively, intentionally and unintentionally—broken the bond of communion, breaching the circle of love.

3. Then we acknowledge with wonder that God has not left us in the condition we have brought upon ourselves, but instead come to us in Jesus Christ to share our life and death with the purpose of reconciling and restoring us to the fold of our spiritual family. Through Jesus God has effectively said to us, "You are my Beloved children. Please come home! Come back into the circle of love and help to expand it."

4. The liturgy proceeds with the story of the Last Supper: "On the night in which he gave himself up for us . . . ." The dreadful divisions of sin were evident right within Jesus' inner circle of disciples. A completely innocent man was framed and betrayed to his killers by an insider. Every person who has ever been wrongly accused or harmed can identify with Jesus, and know that he identifies with them. Our Lord then takes bread, a sign of common life and the intimate bond of table fellowship. He reinterprets it as an emblem of his body to be broken for our sakes. He takes wine, the traditional cup of blessing, friendship, and conviviality, a Jewish symbol of nuptial union, and redefines it as his blood shed for the forgiveness of sin.

5. The invocation of the Holy Spirit upon the elements is "to make us one with Christ, one with each other, and one in ministry to all the world." Here the liturgy acclaims with joy that in Christ we are restored to the original unity of creation and rightful place in the household of God.

6. We then name the sacrament "this holy mystery." In Christ's self-offering to us we find our spiritual healing and renewal. The goal, expressed in prayer, is to "go into the world in the strength of your Spirit, to give ourselves for others." Our unity with Christ grounds our unity and peace with each other in a communion that reveals God's reign among us.

The gift of God's forgiveness offers us the possibility of reconciliation. Reconciliation in turn makes possible restoration to the joy of communion in the glorious circle of God's everlasting love. This is not pie-in-the-sky theology. It is the stuff of real life. Because Holy Communion makes forgiveness a reality to us, forgiveness can now mend our human communion and make vital community possible once again.

Forgiveness Makes Communion Possible

As God's forgiveness of us makes possible reconciliation and restored communion between us, our forgiveness of one another can restore and re-create human community. Communion is not only the ground and means, but also the goal of forgiveness. All three facets of this connection may be clearly seen in the text of Colossians 1:15-20, which proclaims the supremacy of Christ. Early on we noted the original communion of "all things in heaven and on earth . . . created through him and for him" (verse 16). The divine goal becomes clear in verse 20: "and through him God was pleased to reconcile to himself all things, whether on earth or in heaven." Communion as the means is revealed at the end of this verse, "making peace through the blood of his cross."

God's project in this world is reconciliation and restored communion; forgiveness is the path to that end. Our forgiveness of each other allows us to participate in God's project for all humanity. Every act of forgiveness, no matter how small, reweaves the frayed fabric of human relationship, rebuilds the intimacy of love, recreates the possibility of communion.

"Forgiveness is a compassionate act. Compassion involves an imaginative understanding that can reach out to identify with another's hurts, even mistakes or bad tempers." That is to say, in forgiving we recognize our human commonality in wounds and weakness. Forgiveness is also expansive. "It radiates, sending light and warmth over everything it reaches, while resentment focuses tightly on itself . . ."[10] That radiant quality communicates an acceptance of all kinds of people as worthy of our love, regardless of who they are.

A story from the U.S. war in Iraq beautifully illustrates the qualities of compassion and expansiveness in forgiveness: A Christian Peacemaker Team was on its way from Baghdad to Amman when the driver lost control of the car and landed in a deep ditch, leaving several in the company badly injured. An Iraqi civilian stopped to help, packing the injured into his car and driving them to nearby Rutba, a town of 20,000 which had been largely destroyed by American and British air strikes only three days before. At the only medical facility still standing, the Americans were warmly welcomed by the staff, and an Iraqi doctor treated the wounded, apologizing for sparse medicine and the fact that the only ambulance that might have transported them to Jordan had been destroyed by the bombs. When the Americans offered to pay for their care, the Iraqis refused. "We treat everyone in our clinic: Muslim, Christian, Iraqi, or American," said the doctor. "We are all part of the same family, you know."[11] An understanding of the spiritual truth of human communion underlay this man's capacity to forgive, even as his enacted forgiveness helped to re-knit the frayed fabric of relationship between two nationalities and, likely, two religions.

Forgiveness makes communion possible once more, just as lack of forgiveness keeps us stuck in alienation and isolation. Withholding forgiveness is a form of control that ironically controls us. We live under the stress of our unresolved pain, fear, anger, and bitterness, making us unhappy with ourselves as well as others and erecting barriers between us and God. If we cannot forgive others, we cannot receive the mercy God would offer us either. Not because God is bent on punishing us, but because an unforgiving heart blocks the gift of grace.[12]

Forgiveness moves us from being stuck in the past to entering a future of new possibilities. This power was well understood by Martin Luther King, Jr. Challenging the oppression of racial discrimination with the non-violent protests of the civil rights movement, he addressed his most bitter opponents with this goal: "One day we shall win freedom, but not only for ourselves. We shall so appeal to your heart and conscience that we shall win *you* in the process, and our victory will be a double victory."[13] Without in any way capitulating to evil or cooperating with injustice, King desired reconciliation with his enemies, not mere victory over them. His great future hope lay in the vision of a just, equitable, and peaceful world that he called the beloved community. He saw forgiveness as a necessary tool in building this community, a means of repairing human communion.

King's vision is echoed in Desmond Tutu's assessment of the fruits of the Truth and Reconciliation Commission in post-apartheid South Africa: "It is quite incredible the capacity people have shown to be magnanimous—refusing to be consumed by bitterness and hatred, . . . willing to meet in a spirit of forgiveness and reconciliation . . . . We have survived the ordeal and we are realizing that we can indeed transcend the conflicts of the past, we can hold hands as we realize our common humanity."[14]

I find a most moving expression of how forgiveness holds power to restore communion in the following words, written by a Jewish prisoner in a German concentration camp:

> Peace to all men of evil will! Let there be an end to all vengeance, to all demands for punishment and retribution. . . . Crimes have surpassed all measure, they cannot be grasped by human understanding. . . . And so, weigh not their sufferings on the scales of thy justice, Lord, and lay not these sufferings to the torturer's charge to exact a terrible reckoning from them. . . . Put down in favor of the executioners, the informers, the traitors and all men of evil will, the courage, the spiritual strength of the others, their humility, their lofty dignity . . . their love, their ravaged, broken hearts that remained steadfast and confident in the face of death itself. . . . Let all this, O Lord, be laid before thee for the forgiveness of sins . . . let the good and not the evil be taken into account! And may we remain in our enemies' memory not as their victims, not as a nightmare, not as haunting specters, but as helpers in their striving to destroy the fury of their criminal passions. There is nothing more that we want of them."[15]

Forgiveness such as this is an eager participation in God's redemptive grace and promise of transformation. It is the profound healer of shattered communion. And it is possible only because communion is recognizable as the very structure God has woven into the heart of creation and that God continually offers to us in sacramental grace. May we then embrace and offer forgiveness as the incomparable gift it is. May we welcome one another back into the unending, ever-expanding circle of God's love!

Reflection Questions

1. What is your understanding of forgiveness and how would you characterize it? Jot down your own definition, based on experience and reflection.

2. When have you discovered your commonality with others in brokenness and sin? How has this recognition affected your ability to forgive?

3. What connections do you find between Holy Communion and forgiveness? Do you believe that forgiveness can or should be a regular fruit of the sacrament?

4. How have you experienced acts of forgiveness building communion and community?

Notes

1. Henri J.M. Nouwen, "Forgiveness: The Name of Love in a Wounded World," *Weavings* Volume VII, No.2 (Mar/Apr 1992), 10.

2. This quote has been variously attributed to St. Augustine, Meister Eckhart, and Thomas Merton, among others.

3. This (last phrase only) comes from Mary Gordon, "The Fascination Begins in the Mouth," excerpted from The New York Times Book Review, June 13, 1993.

4. Anthony Bloom, *Living Prayer* (Springfield: Templegate Publishers, 1966), 19.

5. Nouwen, *Op. Cit.*, 15, 11.

6. Douglas Steere, *Dimensions of Prayer* (Nashville, TN: Upper Room Books, 1997), 69.

7. John Patton, *Is Human Forgiveness Possible? A Pastoral Care Perspective* (Nashville: Abingdon Press, 1985), 12.

8. Kathleen Fischer, *Forgiving Your Family: A Journey to Healing* (Nashville: Upper Room Books, 2005), 12.

9. Nouwen, Op. Cit., p.10

10. Christine Fleming Heffner, "The Gift of Forgiveness," (Cincinnati: Forward Movement Publications, 1993), 4, 5.

11. Recounted by Doug Hostetter, Evanston Mennonite Church pastor and Senior Middle East Correspondent for the American Friends Service Committee in communiqué dated 3/30/03. Cited in Fischer, 26-27.

12. For a more complete exposition of this theme, see Marjorie J. Thompson, "Moving Toward Forgiveness," *Weavings* Mar/Apr 1992, 21-23.

13. Martin Luther King, Jr., *Strength to Love* (Philadelphia: Fortress, 1981), 52.

14. Desmond Tutu, *No Future Without Forgiveness* (New York: Doubleday, 1999), 120. For a concise discussion of the Beloved Community theme, see Marjorie J. Thompson, *Companions in Christ: The Way of Forgiveness*, Participant's Book (Upper Room Books, 2002), chapter 8.

15. Bloom, 17-18.

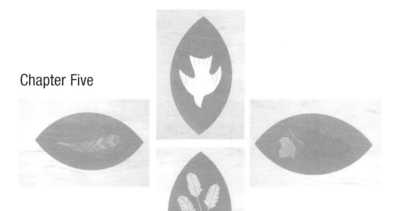

Chapter Five

Table Manners for Peacebuilders
Holy Communion in the Life of Peacemaking

PETER STOREY

"Their sharing of the meal was a living drama of God's dream for the whole world . . . abundant manna for all, abundant mercy for all."[1]

The Communion liturgy we use in South Africa is similar to that used by British Methodists.[2] It closes with the words, "We thank you Lord, that you have fed us in this Sacrament, united us with Christ, and given us a foretaste of the heavenly banquet prepared for all humanity." In order to be Eucharistic peacebuilders, we remember that the deep gift of being fed, the profound experience of being united with Christ is bound to God's vision of a banquet prepared for a healed humankind. The Holy Table is truly a site of peacebuilding and in our search for ways to break through conflict, alienation, and hate, we need to ask how this central act of our worship informs and resources us for our work. What are the "table manners" that we learn in order to be effective peacebuilders?

Each step in the service of Holy Communion contains an important ingredient in our formation as peacebuilders, both individually and corporately. Through it we learn the rhythm that shapes our effort to harmonize with God's purposes.

The Prayer for Purity

The service begins with the Prayer for Purity:

Almighty God, to whom all hearts are open,
all desires known,

and from whom no secrets can be hid;
cleanse the thoughts of our hearts
by the inspiration of your Holy Spirit,
that we may perfectly love you,
and worthily magnify your Holy Name;
through Christ our Lord. **Amen**.[3]

We need to know that, whatever the conflict may be, the one who is working with us in the sacred ministry of peacebuilding has interior access to all the parties involved. We can hold on to this and draw confidence from it. The process does not rely only upon us or the skills we may have gained. God's Spirit can cleanse our thoughts and bring a power beyond ourselves to bear on the limited talents and frail characters of all involved.

Word

The Communion Service is one of *Word* and Table. When we soak ourselves in Scripture we discover that the message of peacebuilding is not located in just a few favorite and obvious passages. When we read with the eyes of those who Jesus calls God's sons and daughters, we will find the call to peacebuilding emerging in all of Scripture. The Bible is the longest love story in the world. It is *all* about this God's passionate search over all the centuries for our hearts, about God's determination to turn enemies into friends. (2 Cor 5:18-19)

We will listen with our hearts and let the stories of our faith help us do something very important: the Word helps us re-imagine what God's peace looks like. I heard recently of a group of Jesuits who had been working, struggling and praying for peace and justice for many years. They were saying that they were not sure they could imagine any longer what God's peace looked like. "The world is such a denial of God's *shalom* that we are not sure that we have the right picture in our minds any longer." That is why Scripture is important to us, because there is a picture there of a "whole universe mended by God."[4] We need to re-vision what God's peace looks like; we need to re-imagine it so that we can declare what *will be*, in order to transform what *is*.

One of our important tasks in South Africa's long struggle for liberation was to help people imagine what they found unimaginable: a South Africa where black and white lived together hand in hand and at peace. It was crucial for the church to incarnate that dream in the life of the Christian community so we could say to an unwilling nation, "There! That is what we mean when we talk about God's future for South Africa! That is the new South Africa." Like Isaiah, we wanted to declare God's new thing. It is very easy once it's in full flower to say, "Ah! There's peace!" But the world needs those who can see peace before it "breaks from the bud" (Isaiah 42:9 NEB), and declare it by the way they live.

Listen to Dietrich Bonhoeffer speaking to a peace council he was attending in 1934:

> How does peace come about? Through a system of political treaties? Through the investment of international capital in different countries? Through the big banks, through money or universal peaceful disarmament in order to guarantee peace? Through none of these for the simple reason that in all of them peace is confused with security and safety. There is no way to peace on the way to safety. For peace must be dared. It is the great venture. It can never be made safe. Peace is the opposite of security. To demand guarantees is to mistrust, and this mistrust in turn brings forth war. To look for guarantees is to want to protect oneself. Peace means to give oneself altogether to the will of God, wanting no security but through faith and obedience laying the destiny of the nations in the hands of Almighty God.[5]

Bonhoeffer then answers his own question by lifting up a vision of a church unafraid, relying utterly on God's word:

> How will peace come so that the whole world will hear, so that all peoples may rejoice? The individual Christian cannot do it. When all around are silent, he can indeed raise his voice and bear witness but the powers of the world stride over him without a word. . . . Only the one great Ecumenical council of the Holy Church of Christ of all the world can speak out so the world, though it gnash its teeth, will have to hear so that the people will rejoice because the Church of Christ in the name of Christ has taken the weapons from the hands of their children, forbidden war, and proclaimed the peace of Christ against the raging world. Why do we fear the fury of the world powers? Why don't we take the power from them and give it back to Christ?

Because we know how Bonhoeffer died his last words in this very brief address are quite haunting. He said:

> We want to give the world a whole word, not a half word, a courageous word, a Christian word. We want to pray that all this word may be given us today. Who knows if we should see each other again in another year?

I wonder when last any of our congregations heard such a passionate and urgent call to peacemaking?

Intercession

In most Christian liturgies, after the word has been proclaimed we turn to *Intercession*. Our intercessions aid God in the work of redemption and only a robust spirituality of engagement with the world, shaped by and reflected in our intercessions, can save our souls from self-absorption.

When I think of intercession, I remember those four men who carried their paralyzed friend to a house where people were "having church"—listening to Jesus. The house was so crowded that when they arrived, all they saw were the backs of the congregation (which is probably the most typical posture of the church towards the world). But they had been bearing their friend's pain in their hearts for long enough, now they bore his body; they were carrying the pain and the struggle and the paralysis of the world, and their intercession required action. They carried him up onto the roof, tore a great hole in it and suddenly, thud! Crash! "Look out below Jesus, we've got work for you!" In a moment of glorious mayhem, there was their friend lying at the feet of Jesus. The pain of the world had hacked its way into the church, to be ignored no longer. That's intercession!

I hope that we will be serious enough peacebuilders, to be prepared to do damage to church property for the love of the world. I hope our intercessionary prayers and actions will break open church roofs—and walls—for the love of the world. I hope we will make it more and more difficult for the church to turn its back on the pain of the world that Jesus came to heal.

The Invitation to the Table

The *Invitation* begins with a very important word for Wesleyans: the word "all." This Table is surely for all. Mary McLeod Bethune founded the first college for African-American women in 1904. I recall a musical about her life in which she sang of the home she had grown up in, a humble cabin in South Carolina. The song title was *There's Always Room for One More*. No matter how small that cabin was, its hospitality seemed to be able to expand for every newcomer. I would like to think that around the Lord's Table, there is always room for one more and that the table manners we are taught here invite us always to make space for another. Hospitality consists of this progressive widening of our hearts.

I confess to a heart that does not widen easily. You may have a similar problem, but Jesus will not stop inviting us, calling us, to expand our hearts. Jesus will want us to make space for friends, he will want us to make space for neighbors, he will want us to make space for strangers, and then—even scarier—he will want us to make space for enemies. In fact, there is absolutely nobody who is not his friend. They may not know it, but he is friend to them already. It grieves me deeply to see part of the church family I belong to obsessed with issues of who may and who may not be called friends of Jesus, and who may and who may not participate in the fullest sense in what this Table stands for, including the vocation to ordained ministry.

I participated with 300 United Methodists at an exciting peacemaking conference in Lansing, Michigan. I had to do quite a bit of speaking and was saying some of the things that I now write, but nothing spoke more powerfully than the concluding worship, when the Lansing Gay Men's Choir arrived to sing. To be more accurate, *some* of them came. They sang original compositions, powerful songs about the pain of how they had grown up and what they had been told about themselves all their lives. There was so much brokenness and hurt, and too much of it had been conveyed or endorsed by the church; yet here they were, standing with incredible courage in front of a body of church people. When they had finished they wanted to scuttle away, but fortunately the organizer stopped them and said, "Please don't go yet, do wait for the prayer." I had to give the benediction and I remember feeling deeply judged by this moment. I said something like, "O God, your unconditional love is eternally expressed by those arms nailed wide open at Calvary. Forgive us that ours are so tightly folded in rejection. Tear our arms open, God, so we can learn to love as you love, to embrace as you embrace."

It is always a little sad to see someone sitting all alone at a restaurant table. We are not meant to eat alone. An important question facing the church is, "Can the Communion Table be the place where we humbly and readily bring not just our worship but our *differences*?" There seem to be two understanding of the Table of the Lord. One is taught mainly by Roman Catholics, but practiced by many Protestants too. It suggests that the Sacrament of our Lord is a confirming ordinance only. It is what you may receive when you're in a "state of grace" and you've got everything right. Wesley was taught that, but he made the heart-expanding discovery that this Table is a "converting ordinance" too, and we may come, not because we've got it right but because we know we desperately need to get it right. Thank God for this converting ordinance, because otherwise, none of us would get to the Table. The invitation is to all.

Some of the most powerful moments in my life have been of Communion in places where people have been divided from one another. I once received a phone call in the early hours of the morning telling me that one of my black clergy in a very racist town sixty miles from Johannesburg had been arrested by the secret police. I got up and drove out there, picked up another minister and then went looking for him. When we found the prison where he was and demanded to see him, we were accompanied by a large white Afrikaner guard to a little room where we found Ike Moloabi sitting on a bench wearing a sweatsuit and looking quite terrified. He had been pulled out of bed in the small hours of a freezing winter morning, and dragged off like that.

I said to the guard, "We are going to have Communion," and I took out of my pocket a little chalice and a tiny little bottle of Communion wine and some bread in a plastic sachet. I spread my pocket handkerchief on the bench between us and made the table ready, and we began the Liturgy. When it was time to give the invitation, I said to the guard, "This table is open to all, so if you would like to share with us, please feel free to do so." This must have touched some place in his religious self, because he took the line of least resistance and nodded rather curtly. I consecrated the bread and the wine and noticed that Ike was beginning to come to life a little. He could see what was happening here. Then I handed the bread and the cup to Ike because one always gives the Sacrament first to the least of Christ's brothers or sisters—the ones that are hurting the most—and Ike ate and drank. Next must surely be the stranger in your midst, so I offered bread and the cup to the guard. You don't need to know too much about South Africa to understand what white Afrikaner racists felt about letting their lips touch a cup from which a black person had just drunk. The guard was in crisis: he would either have to overcome his prejudice or refuse the means of grace. After a long pause, he took the cup and sipped from it, and for the first time I saw a glimmer of a smile on Ike's face. Then I took something of a liberty with the truth and said, "In the Methodist liturgy, we always hold hands when we say the grace," and very stiffly, the guard reached out his hand and took Ike's, and there we were in a little circle, holding hands, while I said the ancient words of benediction, "The grace of our Lord Jesus Christ, the love of God and the fellowship of the Holy Spirit, be with us all."[6]

I wish I could say that Ike was released by an angel of the Lord just then, but that took some days. From that moment, however, the power equation between that guard and Ike was changed forever. God's *shalom* had broken through at that makeshift Table.

Communion is a converting ordinance and when the church is willing to trust what this table can do, people change.

Confession and Absolution

Having prayed for others we must look to our own souls in *Confession.* Building God's *shalom* requires of us an inward journey in which we ask God to surface those attitudes, judgments, hostilities, angers, and hurts within us that could block our usefulness. Jean Vanier talks about coming to terms with the "wolf within."[7]

When things were very bad in South Africa, Trevor Hudson was leading us in retreat. Some of us were under severe pressure, experiencing intimidation and harassment from the secret police. He invited us to name the people "that you really resent, hate and feel alienated from." I didn't have any difficulty writing down "Security Police." Then he said, "Write down all the things about them that you hate," and I had no difficulty with that either, my list was a long one. "Are you sure you are finished? Is there anything else you want to say about them?" he asked, and I made a few more notes. Then came the punchline: "Now I want you to put a line through any of the qualities there that you have not sometime or another discovered in yourself," and I wished my list had been much shorter, because many of the things I hated in those Security Police were also part of my story!

Confession helps us to confront in ourselves the things that we often see more clearly in others. We will not be able to facilitate healing in others until we have at least been honest about the presence of these things in our own lives. The Eucharist invites us to do that, but it doesn't leave us there.

Absolution sets us free to go into conflict situations in the freedom of God's pardon. We go ready to lean into the promise that says, "In the name of Jesus Christ, you are forgiven." Even though we may only be half-whole in our own eyes, we accept the wholeness that God has declared about us and though we cannot fully trust ourselves, we go with the trust that a graceful God is willing to place in us. We go in the confidence that the restoring forgiveness of Jesus is real.

Peace

The words of absolution are followed by the *Peace*. We reach out to embrace one another with "signs of reconciliation and love." Often the people we embrace are strangers: we do not know them, we do not know their stories, nor do we know what hurts, fears, and struggles populate their minds and hearts. We say to them, "The Peace of Christ be with you," and as we speak those words we remember that when Jesus said "*Shalom*," he brought more than a greeting: he imparted the actual gift of his peace: "Peace is my parting gift to you, my own peace, such as the world cannot give. Set your troubled hearts at rest, and banish your fears" (John 14:27 NEB).

On the final occasion when Jesus spoke his gift of *shalom*, his words, "Peace be with you" were followed immediately by a commissioning: "as the Father sent me, so I send you." (John 20:21 NEB). We are invited to take his gift of *shalom* into situations of conflict where sometimes it is the only gift we will have to give to the people we meet there. I have had enough experience to know that when I take a troubled and anxious spirit into such situations, I help not one little bit. I make things worse. Our need to ensure that everything comes out right is the besetting sin of our craft. When I was pressured by my own anxiety to succeed, and to do so in a tight timetable because I had maybe 200 kilometers to drive home late at night from some remote place, that anxiety transferred to those conflicted parties I was working with, making a good outcome almost impossible. We need to hold on like drowning persons to the gift of Christ's peace, and to say to Jesus, "You've given it, I'm going to hold it: I'm going to take you at your word: I'm going to trust your peace."

The Great Thanksgiving

In the ***Great Thanksgiving*** we join the Church Universal, the entire community of believers everywhere, in a glorious act of worship and remembering. We are taken up together into the mighty acts of a God who has broken into time and space and taken the inevitability out of history. As we recall the story of God's saving acts, we move toward becoming integrated again with God's saving purposes for our time and our place. The story has been recounted again and we are part of it in our worship. Through it, by God's Spirit, we are made "one with Christ, one with each other, and one in ministry to all the word . . . ."

Prayer of Humble Access

Sometimes we pray the *Prayer of Humble Access* reminding us that we bring so little to the Table and the mercy that it holds is given by God.

> We do not presume to come to this thy table,
> O merciful Lord,
> trusting in our own righteousness,
> but in thy manifold and great mercies.
> We are not worthy
> so much as to gather up the crumbs under thy table.
> But thou art the same Lord,
> whose property is always to have mercy.
> Grant us therefore, gracious Lord,
> so to partake of this Sacrament of thy Son Jesus Christ,
> that we may walk in newness of life,
> may grow into his likeness, and may evermore dwell in him, and
>   he in us.[8]

We come with little other than good faith. We need to be very careful that we don't put too much trust in our "skills" as if they are weapons, our version of armaments. It is our empty-handedness that may most help us to be useful to the cause of peacebuilding.

I recall a confrontation with the state president of South Africa when church leaders went to try and plead with him to turn his government's *apartheid* policies around. I said, "President Botha, you need to listen to us very carefully because we are the only people who come into your office who don't want your job; most others you listen to have their own power agendas but we are the only ones who come here wanting nothing for ourselves."

That is why the cross of Jesus still speaks the most authentic word in history: because it is spoken out of the heart of someone who wanted nothing but who loved all. God can use our powerlessness to transform. God can do that with the simple elements that we place on the communion table, transforming the wine and bread into sacramental gifts.

Giving the Bread and Cup

So we *Consecrate* and take and eat and drink and we do so in remembrance. Have you ever thought that the opposite of remembering is not forgetfulness. The opposite of remembering is *dismembering*. We live in a dismembered world and it is around this table that we re-member that world, the broken pieces are put together again, God mends the entire universe! This can only happen, however, because Christ has been broken open on the cross. It is only out of his brokenness that healing and mending can come. The breaking of the bread reminds us of our own vocation to be willing to be broken in the cause of wholeness. What a reminder of God's costly ministry! What a reminder of our own!

Dismissal with Blessing

We are then sent forth with a blessing: "Go forth in peace. The grace of the Lord Jesus Christ, and the love of God, and the communion of the Holy Spirit be with you all. Amen"

* * *

These are challenging days and I believe that even more difficult times lie ahead for peacebuilders. The strident voices proclaiming their trust in force and violence for redemption are hard to silence. At the same time it is increasingly difficult to hear the victims of violence out there in the world because soundproof walls have been built. Voices from around the world saying, "please hear us before it is too late," are being shut out. This Table makes world citizens out of all Christians. We are bound to our sisters and brothers everywhere by this Sacrament, and no narrow nationalism is permitted among those who gather to receive it.

The world recalls many important people involved in South Africa's great struggle for liberation, but I want also to remember, with incredible gratitude and a sense of awe, that small body called the Methodist Order of Peacemakers to whom tired and burned out, ashamed and guilty peacebuilders could turn for what the gift of this Table represents. There we could make our deep confession and hear others say, "We know how you feel, but you need also to know that your sins are forgiven." There we gathered around the word and were reminded who we were. There God took our dismembered and shattered faith and put it together again.

It is going to be very costly to go on loving. We need to go from the Table committed to each other, in covenant to pray for one another, resource one another, listen to one another, be in silence with one another, celebrate with one another, hold one another accountable, and act with one another for peace.

Reflection Questions

1. How have you experienced the liturgy of Holy Communion as formative for you life?

2. In what ways have you experienced the liturgy as forming us as peace-builders?

3. Have you experienced moments where the giving of "signs of reconciliation and love" was a genuine movement towards forgiveness and reconciliation? What happened?

4. Have you had an experience like that of Ike Moloabi where Holy Communion broke through to join together those who have been divided?

Notes

1. Daniel Erlander, *Manna and Mercy: A Brief History of God's Unfolding Promise to Mend the Entire Universe* (Mercer Island: The Order of Saints Martin and Teresa, 1992).

2. *The Methodist Service Book,* Revised and Expanded Version, (Methodist Publishing House, London, 1992) B17.

3. From "A Service of Word and Table I," *The United Methodist Hymnal* (Nashville: The United Methodist Publishing House, 1989), 6.

4. A phrase beloved of Daniel Erlander, author of "Manna and Mercy, a Brief history of God's Promise to Mend the entire Universe," copyright 1992, Daniel W. Erlander.

5. Dietrich Bonhoeffer, "The Church and the Peoples of the World" address (1934) in *Dialogue and Resistance* (London: Friends House).

6. Peter Storey, *With God in the Crucible: Preaching Costly Discipleship* (Nashville: Abingdon Press, 2002), 70.

7. In addresses given at the Central Methodist Mission, Johannesburg, November, 1982.

8. From "A Service of Word and Table IV," *The United Methodist Hymnal* (Nashville: The United Methodist Publishing House, 1989), 30.

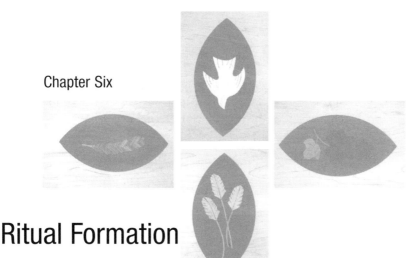

Chapter Six

Ritual Formation
Liturgical Practices and the Practice of Peacebuilding

MARCIA MCFEE

In the midst of a shipwreck on the way to Rome. . .

> *Just before dawn Paul urged them all to eat. "For the last fourteen days," he said, "you have been in constant suspense and have gone without food—you haven't eaten anything. Now I urge you to take some food. You need it to survive. Not one of you will lose a single hair from his head." After he said this, he took some bread and gave thanks to God in front of them all. Then he broke it and began to eat. They were all encouraged and ate some food themselves.(Acts 27:33-36)*

Conflict and Communion

It was a dire situation. Not just because of the tempest sea that raged around them as it had for two weeks, but because of raging tempers that threatened to rip apart their lives faster than the sea. This scene, from the last of Paul's difficult sea voyages, is part of a story with a cast of characters any playwright would relish for the potential for conflict in the storyline. And indeed, conflict is what we get. There are prisoners (including Paul), soldiers who are there to transport them to Rome, and the sailors of the ship who wonder how they ever got stuck with this lot in the first place. After days of relentless and violent battering from the storm, they "gave up all hope of being saved." In the midst of their fear and frustration, soldiers try to kill prisoners and sailors try to abandon the ship in the lifeboat, leaving the rest to die at sea. But Paul thwarts the attempt by telling the centurion, "unless these men stay with the ship, you cannot be saved." In other words, "who is going to drive this thing!?" Or perhaps more to the point, "we're all in this together—no matter how we feel about each other."

And then, in this moment of tempest sea and flaring tempers, Paul urges them *all* to take food—to come to the table and be fed. "You . . ." says Paul, "you who have shared fear, suspense and hunger, share this food, for it will help you survive. For death will not have you." They are invited to the meal not *in spite of* their broken relationships and uncertain future, but *because* at the very core of each person's story, they all share hunger and fear and uncertainty. They are at a threshold of life and death and Paul calls them to not only a meal, but to a ritual. "In front of them all" he takes bread and gives thanks, breaks the bread, and then shows them the way to regain strength for the journey toward life—he eats. They do likewise and are together encouraged.

I am convinced that engaging in ritual together is essential as we navigate broken relationships and uncertain futures. Breaking open our lives—becoming vulnerable to one another and residing in these threshold places of the "not yet"—is essential to peacebuilding. We need rituals of care to navigate the "liminal" places. *Liminality* is a term that has been used by ritual scholars to describe a state that often accompanies ritualized life passages such as initiation rites, rites of marriage or death, and rites which mark changes in relationship, among others. Taken from the root, "limen," which means "threshold," liminality is a state of "betwixt and between."[1] We are not in the same relationship or identity as before. And we are not yet in a newly defined relationship and identity. We entered the story of Paul's shipwreck at a "liminal" place of uncertainty and fear. It was ritual that Paul believed was necessary to give strength and encouragement—an action of choosing life rather than death. Ritual is one way that we pass through this "threshold" state.

I have come to understand that conflict produces liminality. When we are in the "betwixt and betweenness" of conflict, we need ritual processes to help us through it. In conflict, some aspect of relationship which was before, has been breached or broken or changed. But we do not yet see the new thing. We have lost our equilibrium—we have lost our "peace." It is so difficult to be in this kind of liminality, because where we stand in relationship to one another is so vitally connected to our own identity. Relationship is how we know who we are. And so when we are not in "right relationship" it is a deeply disturbing matter. We feel a loss of our sense of self.

The danger is that, because we are so uncomfortable with this liminal state, we won't stay in it long enough to discover a truly new relationship born of honest and difficult reflection on often painful experience. We look for the quick fix, we utilize structures that advocate distancing as a first, rather than last, resort, or we simply turn away because it is too painful. What we often find, however, is that the pain doesn't subside. The quick fix may not be a lasting one. And while distancing may be part of what is needed, feelings of uncertainty may linger if we never come face-to-face. Ritual provides a structure in which to faithfully struggle and search for last-ing solutions. Through ritual, symbolic action "makes real" for us God's restorative possibilities and moves us toward those possibilities. One of the most formative rit-uals for dealing with conflict is contained in the circle process.

I have been privileged to work with Tom Porter and JUSTPEACE several times as a ritual leader at training events for circle processes of restorative justice. As a per-son who studies how ritual shapes and forms us as disciples, I have been deeply moved by the ways in which circle processes facilitate our interactions and provide a safe space for sharing deeply about difficult matters. I have experienced the circle process *as* "communion" in the best sense of that word—a restoration of persons into a wholeness of relationship. These experiences have brought to mind some questions for me: What can we learn from circle processes of restorative justice that would be helpful as we seek to facilitate ritual that becomes the place *par excellence* for dealing openly and honestly with our conflicts? What difference would it make to the ways in which we view and deal with conflict if our worship tutored us—pat-terned us—in the habit of breaking open our lives to one another and sharing our hurts and our hopes?

Ritual Formation

In a recent service of consecration for a new conference building in the Iowa Annual Conference of the United Methodist Church, Bishop Gregory Palmer quoted Winston Churchill, "We shape our buildings and afterwards our buildings shape us." Bishop Palmer then went on to ask the provocative question, "What kind of shape are we in?" So it is with any structure that we inhabit. The kind of "shape" we take on is influenced by the shape of our "practices." The practices of our ritu-als form us—whether they are rituals of coming to work every day in a building with a baptismal fountain at the center, rituals of Holy Communion, or rituals of dealing with conflict, as in the circle process.

Our ritual practices link the forming of our very identity as lovers of justice and seekers of peace. And because of this power, what matters deeply is not just what we say in our rituals, but also how we do what we do. When our ritual practices con-tain within them the embodiment of particular ways of being we, through that practice, become the sorts of persons who are disposed to be *that way.* The act of acknowledging shared experience and then sharing bread together affected, perhaps, the ways in which Paul's fellow shipmates acted when faced with later decisions.

This shaping and forming happens, in part, because our brains think in images or "schemas" that act as organizational maps, helping us navigate our world. The brain likes to categorize experience into these schemas in order to literally "make sense" of the way things are. Because there is so much sensory information coming at us at any one moment, we are what cognitive scientists call, "cognitive misers."[2] We have selective memory by necessity. While we have numerous schemas available to us, only some of them are *easily* accessible to us. These then are the schemas— views of the world and our place in it—that shape our motivations and affect our decision-making.

One of the factors that makes particular schemas "accessible" is the frequency with which we are faced with it.[3] Neuroscientists tell us that the more frequently we visit particular images, the more our memories are strengthened through the strengthening of neural synapses. "Cells that fire together, wire together."[4] When this binding occurs, the connection between the two is strengthened, making the next occasion of firing easier. Memories are made, and the potential for these memories to enter the long-term memory is greatly enhanced, as the frequency of firing escalates. *Remembering* particular schemas structured within the ritual is imperative for the ability of participants to access those constructs outside the ritual. Being neurally facile (having certain neural connections that fire without us having to think about it) comes with repetition. As we associate deeply-felt emotions to ritual practices, the impact of the memory is even more greatly enhanced and these schemas become powerful motivators for our action outside of the ritual.[5] We become the sort of person for whom certain behaviors become "second-nature." This is the neurobiology of habituation, or of "practices."[6] If our repeated ritual practices, like circle processes or Holy Communion, are formative of our lives and our relationships, we must look closely at the images, or "schemas" we create in those ritual practices.

Jesus as "Shape-Shifter"

While not particularly concerned with the neuroscience of ritual formation, Jesus consistently and repeatedly presented his followers with schemas that would reorient their understanding of who they were called to be. Jesus' table practice contained the embodiment of a particular and radical way of being in relationship through which he taught about the reign of God. The rituals he engaged at the table aimed at reshaping popular conceptions of relationship. In our day we may say the phrase "you are what you eat." In the time of Jesus, it was "you are who you eat with." The Greco-Roman and Jewish banquet practices were rituals that communicated social values, ideologies, and social stratification. Dennis E. Smith's book, *From Symposium to Eucharist: The Banquet in the Early Christian World* shows drawings reconstructing "banquet practice" in the ancient world.[7] Rather than the familiar scene from DaVinci's *Last Supper* with Jesus at the center, Smith's drawings show that proper banquet practice placed the honored guest—the "highest ranking" person—at one end of a square configuration of reclining couches with an open space in the middle. Thus, who sat "at the right hand" of the most honored person was "number two" and so on around the seating arrangement. Each person had a place in the order and certainly each one had a role, including servants. Even the lowest ranking person at the "end of the line" ranks above the servant who kneels and washes his feet. Jesus' ministry of table practice redefined many things about the social configurations entrenched in the table practices of his day. Radical hospitality is embodied as he himself takes the place of the "lower than the lowest"—the servant role. Whom he invited to the table and what he did there became a controversial "reshaping" of ritual through which his followers could see what sorts of persons and relationships God was calling them to be and have.

Our communion rituals are, in part, extensions of Jesus' table ministry, and are therefore rituals of redefining relationship and hospitality. They are the symbolic roots of peacebuilding communities—creating right relationship as persons gather together around the table—those who are friends, those who are strangers, even those who are enemies. If we answer this call to the table of Jesus, we can be formed through our rituals as persons working to shift the shape of our own society's dominant images of separation and retribution.

In light of this basic purpose of Jesus' rituals we need to ask, *are* our communion rituals embodying radical hospitality and mutual relationship? Do our rituals tutor us in right relationship, giving us access to reshaped images of the way God calls us to be with each other? Have we embodied the reign of God that we proclaim in our worship in such a vital way that our peacebuilding practices live on beyond our rituals into our everyday relationships? To be sure, our rituals are forming us, but *to what* are we being formed in our worship? For instance, we might ask whether our communion practices actually form us communally. Receiving communion in a single-file line or kneeling at the rail with eyes shut tight is not "wrong," just as understanding communion as partly a moment of opening our individual *selves* to God is not to be replaced. However, if it is the only way we eat at the communion table, we neglect some communal layers of meaning in the ritual. If we hardly ever, or never, reconfigure ourselves and our tables to emphasize the communal aspect of Holy Communion, if we never dare to look into the eyes of our neighbor, find our voices in order to speak honestly of the pain of our lives, of the world and our communities around the table or extend our hands to serve one another, we are missing a large portion of our Eucharistic theology. To redress this neglect of communion as community-forming ritual, we can turn to circle rituals.

Sitting "In Circle"

The circle process of restorative justice can be used in many situations but is often used to facilitate decision-making and healing of relationships in the face of wrongdoing. The *whole* network of persons affected by the wrongdoing—victims, perpetrators, families, friends, colleagues—agree to "sit in circle" (literally) and, one at a time, to voice their hurts and hopes. The process continues at the direction of a steward as many "go-rounds" as it takes to come to a good place for all involved. Its goal is to move from processes of justice-making that are solely retributive to solutions that are restorative of relationship; from the punitive to the curative; from the retaliatory to the reconciliatory. In order to accomplish this, the very structure or "shape" of the ritual shapes its participants. This Native American saying expresses this well: "You can't get to a good place in a bad way."[8]

We need rituals of care that provide safe spaces in which to feel the full range of emotions inherent in conflict, to speak the truth in love, and to come to a healing place. In other words, we need rituals that get us to a "good place in a good way." The circle process is a ritual form created to give us a structure for passing through the liminal state of conflict and guide us in such a way as to include all voices, taking enough time to come to a new and restorative relationship. It is an extended "rite of passage" that moves us through conflict in three stages. There is a beginning ritual and closing ritual that bookend the circle process itself. Each stage is equally important for creating a safe space and facilitating a newness of relationship.

The steward and ritual leader of the circle process opens with a ritual that "sets apart" the space and time as special and sacred. The presence of all participants is acknowledged and affirmed. Introduction of the talking piece (whether it is a feather or Bible or bowl full of some significant and meaningful objects) by having participants pass it around the circle in silence is a way of embodying the reality that all will have access to voicing their perspectives without interruption. This action can also symbolize the willingness and openness of all participants to enter and honor the circle process itself. Words, Scripture, and/or a song may be offered that set a calming tone and provide verbal encouragement based on scripture or other appropriate and meaningful sources. The introduction of a centerpiece—a symbolic object that will remain at the center of the circle throughout the entire process—can provide metaphors to affirm what will happen in the process. For instance, broken pieces of pottery set alongside a chunk of molding clay can acknowledge both the presence of brokenness and the possibility of a new creation. Lighting a candle may signify the illumination that is hoped for. A living plant may offer a sign of the possibility of growth and renewal. Salt, an ancient preservative, can function as a sign of a covenant agreement of confidentiality between participants. Perhaps a loaf and cup will reside in the center that will be used later in a Service of Word and Table to mark this passage. Appropriate symbols will differ from situation to situation. One of the things I have discovered about the power of symbol in this context is its many layers. A ritual leader may suggest meanings but often it will be the participants themselves, as they search for words to describe their feelings, who will uncover, layer by layer, the depth of the metaphors. Participants help open up the symbol and, likewise, sometimes it is the symbol that helps open up the words and feelings of the participants when words are difficult to find.

The second stage is the circle process itself. In experiencing this process, it has struck me that this is truly a kind of "liturgy" in the basic sense of that word. *Liturgy* literally means "work of the people." In this process, it is the people themselves who name and define past, present, and future realities and relationships. Past relationships that have been broken and lost are remembered and mourned. Present pain and uncertainty that is defining relationships because of wrongdoing are named and sometimes cried over, raged over, sighed over. One of the most fascinating things to me about the power of the ritual of circles is that because the structure itself models respect for all voices, the voices themselves take on an almost reverent tone most of the time—a respectful demeanor. Even in the midst of heated and painful emotions, the power of being heard without interruption allows a kind of honest expression that facilitates listening rather than shutting off. The circle facilitates speaking of and hearing the most difficult of things. Reflections on understandings, misunderstandings, responsibility, and accountability begin to redefine present reality and finally, with the careful urging of the steward of the circle, naming of future relationship is attempted. "What is needed to address the harm and bring us to healing?" It is, indeed, very hard "work." And it is certainly "of the people."

Finally, the third stage of passage through the conflict is that of the closing ritual. The steward confirms a plan for restoration and healing as defined by the group, names the new relationships (at the very least we are persons who have heard each other) and then leads the people in a symbolic action that embodies the exit from liminal states to a new "state of being" together. Because the circle process may take more than one day, this last step is reserved for the time when all feel they have come to such a state of being.

Shaping Relationship

The circle process creates important symbolism in its very form. Symbols help us address our yearning to make the mysterious, the ineffable, or the seemingly impossible more real, more tangible. So, the *possibility of reconciliation* in the midst of conflict is made "more real" to us the minute we engage in the circle. All persons in a circle are equidistant from the center and everyone has equal visual access to one another. This creates a non-hierarchical relationship and fosters the sense that all are equally accountable to the process and the outcome. The role of the community and the truth of an action's effect on that community, not just on victims and perpetrators, is embodied in the shape and process of sitting in circle. The circle is a symbol of not only what "could be" but what, at the same time, *is* an act of mutuality in the very process. Circles help us try new configurations on for size. In the circle process we create a space in which we begin to pattern our very bodies to the possibility that we will be restored to a new form of right relationship as we grapple with the consequences of actions and become mutually accountable. While the process is anything but easy, by sitting in circle we are more likely to arrive at a solution that comes out of our having dealt honestly with our *interconnectedness*. Sitting in circle is a practice whereby we begin to view relationships within a schema of the connectedness of all persons and actions. We begin to see the world beyond the circle in this same light. This is exemplified by a statement by Michael from the Roca community near Boston[9] that uses circles with at-risk youth.

> The more you are in circle, physically sitting in circle, the more
> you get to be in circle when you're not in circle.[10]

We see how the pattern of the circle—the ritual of the circle as it is repeated over time— infuses Michael's interactions outside of the time and place of the actual circles. He is given a schema—or image—that becomes "second-nature" for him. His life becomes steeped in this model of mutuality.

As we engage in the practice of sharing food and forgiveness, offering honesty and receiving grace through our ritual of Holy Communion week after week, we internalize this paradigm of relating and carry it into the world where it can mold our relationships outside of the ritual.[11] To rephrase Michael's wisdom: "The more you are in Communion, physically participating in Communion, the more you get to be in communion when you're not in Communion." As Holy Communion takes a more central place in our worship practices, it becomes a ritual that shifts the shape of our relating, calling us to a social order based in the example of Jesus.

Liturgy as the Deepest Things We Know

The practice of sitting in circles of restorative justice has much to offer us, I believe, as we reflect about our own liturgical practice. Celebrating Holy Communion in an actual circle configuration is one way to bring the communal dimension of Eucharist to the forefront of our practice. This may happen in small group settings of Word and Table outside of the Sunday service that can incorporate actual dialogue around the circle about difficult issues.[12] Additionally, the power of the circle may be experienced within a congregational worship setting with larger attendance by creating several smaller circle configurations after the Eucharistic prayer and serving one another the communion elements. Holy Communion, understood as a practice of peacebuilding (whatever the context), takes on significant depth as we look into each other's eyes and direct our attention and intentions toward one another. The invitation to the table becomes an invitation to reshape our relationships. Confession and forgiveness opens us to the possibility that we are mutually accountable to the whole. Passing the peace, giving thanks for the saving relationship of God through Christ, and asking the Holy Spirit to transform us so that we might be bread for the world takes on special dimensions as the circle is broken open and widened with new faces and sometimes challenging relationships.

However, reflecting on what circles of restorative justice teach us sparks some broader questions regarding the whole of our liturgies as well. Do we understand our liturgy as a place where transformation can happen? Do we expect transformation from our liturgies? Do our words and songs and symbols portray this possibility and carefully set a tone and safe space where that can occur? My friend Nina Reeves says to me when I see her only occasionally, "Let us speak about the deepest things we know." Indeed. Do we invite our communities of worship to speak about the "deepest things?" Do we invite dialogue at all? Do we believe that God invites us to speak honestly, in the context of our rituals of worship, of pain and uncertainty? To lament? Karen Lebacqz names the consequences of avoiding conflict,

> Bland worship avoids both pain and joy. In our anesthetized life, we are so afraid of pain that, in our desire to mute suffering, we sometimes stifle joy. The gospel is good news. But it is good news in the midst of pain and suffering . . . . If we try to avoid the pain and suffering, we will also not be able to hear or embody the gospel. We will not incarnate the Word.[13]

I was asked to design and lead worship for the meeting of a regional body who had, the year before, voted to merge two conferences into one. As is true with most mergers of any sort, conflicting feelings surfaced during the decision-making process. After the decision had been made to merge, the conflict and difficult feelings lingered on. After speaking with several people at the heart of the conflict, I knew that to simply celebrate the creation of the new conference without recognition of the "liminal" state that lingered through feelings of uncertainty and anger would be a mistake. We needed to acknowledge the depth of emotion in order to move toward that celebration. During the first day of the meeting, I invited anyone who wished to do so to spend some time in a meditative ritual space set apart for this purpose and write their hopes and/or fears about the direction of the conference on pieces of paper. I then fashioned these into the Prayers of the People in preparation for our Service of Word and Table. The statements were read by someone recognized in the conference as a healing presence, along with improvised music by a jazz musician and improvised movement—idioms that, when allowed the full range of expression, can often speak what words cannot. What was offered in the statements was exactly what was asked for—some were hopeful and some were expressions of deep pain. There was harmony and dissonance, soaring gestures as well as heaviness of heart and limbs. The prayer asked that God bless it all. We acknowledged that there was room at the Table for all of it. That indeed, the Table was *the* place for all of it. In that moment, the fullness of that community was taken up, blessed, broken open, and shared. And persons who especially felt that their positions had been dismissed by the decisions made, saw that they would continue to have a voice and a place at the Table.

To engage ritual practices of naming conflict, and breaking bread in the midst of these "deep things," is to be faithful. To do this is not "magic" in the sense that it always accomplishes a predictable outcome. Even after Paul's ritual moment of offering bread in the midst of tempest sea and raging tempers, soldiers still wanted to kill prisoners to keep them from escaping. But, some hearts had been changed, some attitudes shifted, and the lives of the prisoners were spared. All who had eaten together swam together to the shore. Those who could not swim shared planks of the broken ship to help them to the shore. Yes, the broken pieces proved to be what saved their lives.

As peacebuilders, as stewards of the Table and of circles, we are called to follow Jesus' practice of table fellowship—reshaping relationship and the ways we deal with our conflict. Peacebuilders are to issue, as Paul did, the call to the fourfold pattern of Christ at the table. The call to "take"—the invitation to bring our brokenness to the table, to touch it, to deal with it, to take it up. The call to "bless"—to name the table as the appropriate place, the sacred place to bring conflict and to bless that conflict, and to understand the liminal places as blessedly re-creative. The call to "break"—the invitation to break open our lives and feelings to each other, to speak of the deepest things we know. And the call to "share"—empowering *all* voices in the process of healing. To say to each other, "we as a community cannot do without *your* piece . . . we cannot do without your *peace.*"

Reflection Questions

1. Imagine, or literally sit with your group in, the configuration of a typical courtroom. Explore what the spatial configuration says about relationship and the process of coming to a resolution. Then imagine, or sit in, a circle. What are the differences? What does the circle represent and bring into being about relationship? Now, reflect on the different configurations you have experienced in Holy Communion rituals. Since often "actions speak louder than words," what do the ways in which the ritual is enacted say about relationship? What feels congruent? What might be missing if only one manner of coming to the table is practiced?

2. What "liminal" places of passage are you experiencing now in your life or in the life of your community? Do you have rituals of care where change and conflict can be addressed in safe and welcoming ways? Can you imagine how communion might become a ritual of care that helps encourage and sustain the community even, and especially, in the midst of that conflict and change?

Notes

1. Victor Turner, *The Ritual Process: Structure and Anti-Structure* (New York: Aldine De Gruyter, 1969), 94-96.

2. David Kertzer, *Ritual, Politics and Power* (New Haven: Yale University Press, 1988), 80.

3. Kertzer, 80.

4. Joseph LeDoux, *The Emotional Brain: The Mysterious Underpinnings of Emotional Life* (New York: Simon & Schuster, Inc., 1996), 214.

5. For more on the role of emotions, see Antonio Damasio, *The Feeling of What Happens: Body and Emotion in the Making of Consciousness* (New York: Harcourt Brace, 1999).

6. For more on the neuroscience of ritual practices, see "Forming Disciples: How Theologies/Ethics are Lodged in the Body," in Marcia McFee, *Primal Patterns: Ritual Dynamics, Ritual Resonance and Polyrhythmic Strategies for the Forming of Disciples,* (Ph.D. Diss., Graduate Theological Union, 2005), 47-94.

7. Dennis E. Smith, *From Symposium to Eucharist: The Banquet in the Early Christian World* (Minneapolis: Augsburg Fortress Press, 2003), 15-17.

8. As quoted in Carolyn Boyes-Watson, "Healing the Wounds of Street Violence: Peacemaking Circles and Community Youth Development," *Community Youth Development Journal* Vol 2, No. 4 (Fall 2001).

9. Roca is a multicultural, youth, family, and community development organization. Download "Holding the Space: www.rocainc.org/pdf/circle.pdf by Dr. Carolyn Boyes-Watson, a document that describes more about peacemaking circles at Roca at www.rocainc.org.

10. From a presentation by representatives of ROCH at the Restorative Justice Institute sponsored by Boston Theological Institute, June 19, 2003.

11. *This Holy Mystery* encourages United Methodists to reclaim a weekly practice of Word *and Table. This Holy Mystery: A United Methodist Understanding of Holy Communion* (Nashville: Discipleship Resources, 2005), 14.

12. See William Johnson Everett's chapter in this book for an example of a community who practices Holy Communion in a circle configuration.

13. Karen Lebacqz, *Word, Worship, World, and Wonder: Reflections on Christian Living* (Nashville: Abingdon Press, 1997), 72-73.

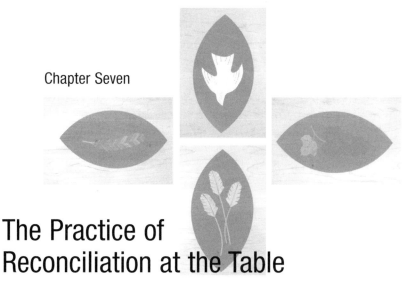

Chapter Seven

The Practice of
Reconciliation at the Table

THOMAS W. PORTER

> *"You prepare a table before me in the presence of my enemies; you anoint my head with oil; my cup overflows." (Psalm 23:5)*

> *"What do you think? If a shepherd has a hundred sheep, and one of them has gone astray, does he not leave the ninety-nine on the mountains and go in search of the one that went astray? And if he finds it, truly I tell you, he rejoices over it more than over the ninety-nine that never went astray. So it is not the will of your Father in heaven that one of these little ones should be lost. If another member of the church sins against you, go and point out the fault when the two of you are alone. If the member listens to you, you have regained that one. But if you are not listened to, take one or two other along with you, so that every word may be confirmed by the evidence of two or three witnesses. If the member refuses to listen to them, tell it to the church; and if the offender refuses to listen even to the church, let such a one be to you as a Gentile and a tax collector. Truly I tell you, whatever you bind on earth will be bound in heaven, and whatever you loose on earth will be loosed in heaven. Again, truly I tell you, if two of you agree on earth about anything you ask, it will be done for you by my Father in heaven. For where two or three are gathered in my name, I am there among them." (Matthew 18:12-20)*

In chapter one, I asked what it might look like if we truly remembered the Last Supper, deeply internalized its lessons and practiced, as Jesus did, naming our conflicts in the context of receiving and sharing the bread and wine. What might it mean to us, to the spirit in which we engage each other, including our enemy, and to our understanding of Holy Communion, to name our conflicts at the Table, work through the conflicts to a good place and do so with the understanding that we would then receive and share bread and wine? This chapter will explore some concepts of conflict transformation that might guide us in the practice of, as well as present examples of attempts to practice, reconciliation at the Table.

I am not describing a process that would take place on Sunday morning in the context of an hour-long worship service of Holy Communion, although I have heard of services where people were moved to walk across the aisle and reconcile with a fellow member in such a service. All of the experiences I will describe took time, all the time that was needed. My hope is that these experiences, however, will begin to inform the Table of Reconciliation on Sunday morning, when the people remember the times when the Table was the context for relational healing. My hope is that these experiences begin to inform all the tables in our lives.

I describe a process within the community of baptized Christians. I hope that this process might inform other tables where we come together to seek a good place with our neighbors regardless of their religious affiliation.

Finally, I should point out two primary challenges to what I am suggesting about practice at the Table. The first challenge is not to make "This Holy Mystery," which is a work of salvation, simply a tool or a formulaic means to an end. We need to recognize that this is God's Table of Reconciliation, while recognizing that God has prepared it for us and that God calls us at this Table to be reconcilers. The second challenge is to do no harm to victims and offenders at the Table by using the ritual to be manipulative or coercive, to force them to forgive or to reconcile when they are not ready. We need to keep both of these challenges in mind as we try to practice reconciliation at the Table.

The Journey to the Table: Lessons Learned

My own understanding of the Table of Reconciliation and the practice of reconciliation is the product of a long journey, to which I alluded in the Introduction. My journey began with my experiences as a trial lawyer and chancellor for my annual conference and with my growing recognition of the problems created by the adversarial retributive justice system for dealing with conflict and harm. I experienced this not only in the courtroom, but in our churches and in our communities. I began to see the adversarial retributive system of our courtroom as the framework for most of our practices in dealing with conflict and harm in this world. I began to see how ultimately destructive this system is to our communities, our churches and our world. I saw how understandings of retributive justice distorted our understanding of God and our theories of God's atonement, something that William Everett addresses, and how it was contrary to what Jesus taught and how he lived and died. Jesus taught us that the only way out of cycles of woundedness, retribution, and violence is the way of forgiveness. The search for a better way led me through the study and practice of mediation to a study of the Truth and Reconciliation Commission in South Africa and then to the study and practice of restorative justice through the circle process. The lessons I learned on this journey have profoundly affected my understanding of the practice of reconciliation at the Table as well as my appreciation for the sacred space and time of Holy Communion: its gift of an alternative to our retributive understanding of justice through a new experience of forgiveness, reconciliation and restorative justice.

The Need for an Alternative to the Adversarial, Retributive Justice Model

On the first day of my practice as a lawyer, I found a tape waiting for me from my new boss. He was out of the office on a month-long trial. On the tape, he gave me some practical advice about trial practice. He explained that each of the partners in the office had a different style. He described the differences between one of the Catholic partners in the firm and a Quaker partner. He described the Catholic partner, who attended Mass every morning, as a pugilist. On cross-examination, he would feint and then punch and bludgeon the witness to a bloody pulp. He described the Quaker as a gentle man. His style of cross-examination was different. He used a stiletto. Because of the soft-spoken nature of the Quaker, the witness would never see the stiletto coming and would sometimes not even know when it entered between the ribs. The result, my boss said, was the same with both approaches. After the cross examination there was a pool of blood under the witness chair.

I can remember being a little shocked, but also amused as I pictured the Quaker with the stiletto. I wanted to be Atticus Finch, the gentleman litigator. I did not think of myself as using a stiletto. In practice I discovered that I was a Methodist with a stiletto. My boss was simply being honest about the process. Even when you want to do it differently, doesn't the adversarial retributive system cause Quakers and Methodists to use stilettos?

Retributive justice is a punishment system. The question for retributive justice is "Who did it?" and "How should they be punished?" For that reason it is necessarily an adversarial system.

Over the course of twenty-five years of trying cases, I developed an increasing respect for the nobility of being a legal counselor and advocate for people in conflict. My lover's quarrel, which became more intense over time, was with the adversarial, retributive system. This is the model we have adapted in the United Methodist Church for church trials. Even in the political life of the Church we have become caught up in this system by becoming adversarial in our relations with each other and by our desire to punish those who "harm" us or with whom we disagree.

I began to realize that the adversarial system is not conducive to healing or restoring relations, to building community, or to growth and learning and real human transformation. This system offers little opportunity for empathy and recognition or apology and forgiveness. In fact, little encounter or dialogue happens between the parties. This system of dealing with harm and conflict is not even very good at getting at the truth. The adversarial system, with painful retributive consequences for losing, creates an atmosphere for defensiveness, half-truths, and lying.

Is there another understanding of justice, another way other than the adversarial one for dealing with conflict and harm in this world? I wanted to find a way that was consistent with the teachings and practice of Jesus and was conducive to the practice of the ministry of reconciliation.[1]

The Importance of Collaborative Processes

Through the study and practice of mediation, I discovered what happens when you move from the two adverse tables in the courtroom to one table where people talk with each other and together work to resolve their problems. I learned that resolving conflicts has to do with relationships and working toward restructuring relationships, with the participants empowered to transform their own problems and conflicts. I learned that mediation shifts the primary focus from the past to the future, from facts to the relationship, from establishing liability or fault to restructuring the relationship, and from winners and losers to a mutual agreement.

I will never forget the feeling of the shift in consciousness when I moved from approaching parties in a dispute from the vantage point of a litigator to that of a mediator. I began to experience a connectedness, a relationship with both parties and an experience of empathy and recognition with both. I liked looking to the future. I liked restoring to people a sense of power and control over their own conflicts. I liked the process of dialogue more than the process of debate. For this trial lawyer, the experience of mediation was like a religious experience, experiencing the power of bringing people together in a way that enabled them to come to a good place together

The values and practices of mediation must inform our practice at the Table. Mediation was, however, just the first step in my journey. After mediating for some time, I began to understand that I had discovered an alternative to the adversarial system, but that I had not discovered an alternative to retributive justice. The adversarial system serves retributive justice. What justice does a collaborative process serve? I served for many years as the president of the Council of Religion and Law as well as the chair of the editorial board of the *Journal of Law and Religion*. I worked with law professors and theologians on the relation between religion and law, including what each had to teach us about justice. It was in South Africa in 1997, studying the Truth and Reconciliation Commission and the work of the Centre for Conflict Transformation at the University of Cape Town, that I began to see an alternative.

The Lessons of the Truth and Reconciliation Commission

In South Africa, I felt like I was coming home. My sense is that the world is just beginning to understand the profound lessons that Nelson Mandela, Bishop Desmond Tutu, and other South Africans have taught us: lessons about the importance of relationships and the need for reconciliation, about the power of the telling and hearing of stories, about the role of forgiveness and apology in relationships, and about restorative justice.

Ubuntu and the Body of Christ

The first lesson, for me, was an understanding of the concept of *ubuntu*. This is a basic comprehension of human nature and community that is shared by most Africans. This is the belief that we are the creation of our relationships, that we are interdependent. I am only a person through other persons. Instead of saying with Descartes, "I think, therefore I am," we say "I participate, therefore I am." When I dehumanize you, I dehumanize myself. Life is about relationships, the restoring of relations and the building of community. Our humanity, our individuality, comes into its own in community. The community envisioned by *ubuntu* is a community that affirms the individual. In fact, many tribes in Africa were communities based on consensus decision-making.

As I listened to people in South Africa, I realized that this is what I had been taught about the body of Christ. This is *shalom* or right relations. Later I realized that this understanding of *ubuntu* is at the heart of any understanding of restorative justice and Holy Communion.

The Power of the Telling and Hearing of Stories

The second lesson learned in South Africa was the power of the telling and hearing of stories, primarily for the victim, but also for the offender. I listened to the stories victims told, in a safe space, with all the feelings being expressed as well as the facts, with people who came to listen, not cross-examine. We saw Bishop Tutu cry after hearing the stories, something judges are not supposed to do. Judith Herman, a Cambridge psychologist who has written on trauma and the healing of trauma, is right when she says, "The recitation of facts without the accompanying emotions is a sterile exercise, without therapeutic effect."[2] I learned that the telling of these stories under these circumstances could be a healing experience for the victims. I also saw the effect of these stories on the perpetrators and those who stood by silently. Many were moved by these stories. They began to see what effect their actions had on another human being. The story has power to speak truth and open up the hearts and souls of people. These stories are very different from the cross-examined, manipulated lawyer stories told on the witness stand, and these stories ultimately get at truth, I believe, in a much more profound and healing way.

I will never forget Father Michael Lapsley, a white Anglican priest who had been exiled from South Africa because of his anti-apartheid activity. After Mandela was released from prison, Father Lapsley was preparing to return to South Africa when he received in the mail a church publication with a letter bomb inside. He was fortunate that he only lost his hands and one eye. He is now Director of the Institute for the Healing of Memories and leads Healing the Memories workshops. Participants include whites, both English and Afrikaners, blacks and coloreds. They watch a drama that includes something for everyone. As they talk about the drama they begin to tell their stories about their experiences under apartheid. There are many things that happen over this weekend, but in the end they create a liturgy, which weaves together all their stories. In the telling and hearing of the stories the participants move from shame and humiliation to a new sense of dignity. This is the beginning of a process where the truth is told, memories are healed, bridges are built that overcome social distance, and relationships are created where none existed before. A new future is created. Is this a vision of what can and should happen at the Table of Holy Communion?

Apology and Forgiveness

In South Africa I also began to see in the political arena the embodiment of the spiritual truth that the way to restored relations or reconciliation involves apology and forgiveness. As Bishop Tutu said, not just to the religious community but also to the whole human community, "There is no future without forgiveness."[3] Forgiveness is the only way we can break the cycle of retribution and violence. Here we see the reality that forgiveness is communal as well as personal.

Restorative Justice

Finally, as I talked with people in South Africa, including lawyers, I began to hear more and more about restorative justice. What folks in South Africa had learned is that retributive justice is inconsistent with the movement towards truth and reconciliation, towards building community. This is not to say that justice is not being served when you seek truth and reconciliation, but that a new understanding of justice is needed. I began to see an alternative to retributive justice, something Bishop Tutu and others called restorative justice. This justice focused not just on those who created harm, but on victims and the community as well. The focus was on harm and addressing the harm, first to victims, then to the community as a whole, and finally to the offender. Here in this political arena I began to see what biblical justice looks like in practice. I also began to see that restorative justice has importance beyond the criminal justice system, beyond the civil justice system, beyond the law. It governs all our relations. Isn't this the justice of the Table of Holy Communion?

The Principles of Restorative Justice

After returning from South Africa, I studied at Eastern Mennonite University with Howard Zehr, the father or grandfather of the restorative justice movement, now an international movement. This is where it all came together for me: the goals of mediation or similar methods of dealing with disputes, *ubuntu*, the importance of relationships, the power of telling and hearing stories, and the role of forgiveness and apology in the creation of a new relationship.

Zehr taught me that restorative justice has three primary principles: a focus on harm, on accountability, and on engagement. Unlike the retributive system, which focuses on the violation of rules, restorative justice focuses on the harm created—harm to victims, the community, and often to offenders as well. Victims and their needs become central.

In this light, accountability takes on new meaning. "Too often we have thought of accountability as punishment—pain administered to offenders for the pain they have caused. Unfortunately, this often is irrelevant or even counterproductive to real accountability." For Zehr, real accountability means being encouraged to understand and "to begin to comprehend the consequences of one's behavior. Moreover, it means taking responsibility to make things right insofar as possible, both concretely and symbolically."[4]

Retributive justice affirms that our actions have consequences, but I began to see that punishment in the retributive system is an imposed accountability, which generally makes the offender see himself or herself as a victim without moral responsibility. How different this is from the personal acceptance of accountability by the offender! This is an accountability that means something to the victim, that has the power to transform the offender, and that serves the needs of the community. This accountability comes out of dialogue, out of telling and hearing stories, and gives the offender the possibility of being reintegrated into a relationship with the victim and the community. There is real accountability which allows the offender to recover his or her status as a moral agent.

The third major principle of restorative justice is engagement. This is not an adversarial exchange between lawyers, but a real engagement or dialogue among the parties trying to seek an outcome that makes things right.

Restorative Justice is the story of the parable of the lost sheep in Matthew 18: seeking out, restoring, and rejoicing. No one is to be lost. In this chapter, Jesus also gives very practical advice on how this restoration will take place, with the victims having the moral authority to confront the offender, to ask for accountability, and to seek healing. The offender has the moral responsibility of conversion, and accountability leading to healing. The journey of the offender is to listen, to understand, to acknowledge the offense (confess), and make things right (repent). If this is done, Jesus says that the offender will be restored to community. The restoration is always met with great rejoicing, as in the parable of the lost sheep. God is present on this journey with everyone.

The Practice at the Table

This journey brought me finally to the Table of Holy Communion and practicing what I learned at the Table. What does the practice look like, after all the preparation has been done and everyone has agreed to come to the Table? What follows is just one person's practice and this has evolved over time. You will discover refinements and even better ways as you begin your own practice at the Table.

The circle process ideally takes place at a round communion table, as suggested by William Everett, with everyone sitting on the "same side of the table." The circle symbolizes our interconnection and interdependence. The circle also affirms the collective wisdom of the participants with everyone having equal voice and equal responsibility for the outcome. The circle is a symbol of the community we are trying to create.

Opening Ritual

After a greeting that recognizes each person and the courage and hope that brought them to the Table and after naming what the focus of our conversation will be, we recognize that we are at the Table of Holy Communion. The Table is set with the cup and the bread. We recognize that we are in the presence of the one who loves each one of us, who forgives, who reconciles and who can guide us in the challenging journey of dealing with our own conflicts and experiences of harm. We talk about the *Invitation*, about how we are at the Table because we would like to live in peace with each other, recognizing how hard this can be and that this peace must be a just peace. We recognize that we are going to confess the way we are by sharing our stories with each other before God. We agree together that, regardless of the outcome, at the end of our time together we will receive the gift of the bread and wine, needing it as much if we fail as we do if we succeed. Being in this sacred space, in most situations, immediately creates a different and more constructive dynamic in the circle. We pray for guidance.

The Relational Covenant, the Talking Piece

The next step involves agreeing on a relational covenant that deals with confidentiality, with how we are going to talk and listen to each other and with our commitment to stay with the process until we all agree that nothing more can be done. This covenant creates safety and gives everyone a common project to work on together, a project where all participants can share their values as well as their hopes. We have all talked about the covenant before we gather, but we always ask if additions or corrections should be made to guide us in how we treat each other.

At the heart of the relational covenant is agreement on the role of the talking piece and also agreement as what the talking piece will be. Circles use a talking piece, something of significance to the group, to empower deep listening and speaking that encourages dialogue. Part of the relational covenant is that participants speak only when they hold the talking piece. The talking piece is passed in order around the circle. Everyone has an equal opportunity to be heard without interruption and commentary. This process frees everyone else to listen. The participants usually agree to the Bible as a talking piece.

POWERFUL QUESTIONS AND THE JOURNEY TO A GOOD PLACE

One of the most important tasks as steward is to ask a powerful question that opens up people's stories and their dreams and hopes. I like to start with a question about each person's hope for the circle. The Bible is then passed around the circle, from left to right. When it returns to me, I then summarize the contributions of the circle and then ask a second question that moves us deeper into responding to the focus of the circle. All of this is about sharing our stories, stories that comprise an authentic *Confession* of the way we are. When the conversation is going well, I often put the Bible on the Table and just call on those who want to speak, maintaining the spirit of the talking piece and making sure we have everyone in the conversation. As the needs and interests become clear to everyone, we let our imaginations go in exploring options to meet these needs and interests. This is where great energy and creativity is released.

At the end of the conversation, I then summarize the consensus or, if there is no consensus, what has been accomplished and what has not been accomplished. Our hope is that all of this leads to the possibility of offering one another signs of reconciliation and love.

THE CELEBRATION OF HOLY COMMUNION

We then close with Holy Communion, even if we were not able truly to offer each other signs of reconciliation and love. All of this must be done in a way that is not manipulative, and does not trivialize either peoples harm or the sacrament of Holy Communion. All of this is highly contextual, depending on the focus for the circle at the Table.

Practice

A TABLE FOR CONVERSATION ABOUT IMPORTANT ISSUES

We can imagine that the meals with Jesus not only involved food but good and passionate conversation. Margaret Wheatley, a woman who has worked over her lifetime with leadership issues, says that the world will be changed through simple, honest, human conversation around issues about which we are passionate.[5] She mentions two women around their kitchen table who decided they wanted to do something about landmines. They started an international movement and received the Nobel Peace Prize for their efforts. William Everett will relate how his worshiping community gets together every Sunday night around the Table—a round communion table—to feast at the Table and to reflect on the word in the context of an issue of importance to the community.

I have been encouraged by how large groups have addressed their issues through circles process at the Table. For example, the ministers of a conference came together to affirm the best moments of their annual conference and also to deal with all that was getting in the way of experiencing more of these moments. Four hundred people came together and worked in circles of ten, which reported verbally and in writing to the whole group. The day began with setting the Table for communion, continued with collecting the wisdom of the ministerd, and ended with communion.

A TABLE FOR HEALING

In our church, a family was having problems dealing with the drug addiction of their son. They expressed the need for help. Members of the community came together around the Table. Everything was named. Everything was discussed. Members of the church became part of this families healing journey, agreeing in different ways to help. Everyone found that their lives and issues were being touched in healing ways as well. The non-party participants in these processes often talk about how they have been helped by the process, how they are moved to deep levels within themselves as they consider their own woundedness as they walk with those who have asked for healing at the Table. You can imagine how couples, families and members might bring their needs for relational healing to the Table.

In different ways, we are all in need of healing in our relations. In the basement of our churches, at the twelve step program, people recognize their need for help. They are honest. They are vulnerable. They know how needy they are. What if this spirit moved from the basement into our sanctuaries around the Table?

A TABLE FOR DEALING WITH HARM

At the same time as the General Conference of the United Methodist Church was approving *This Holy Mystery*, the delegates approved just resolution practices, informed by restorative justice principles, for our grievance procedures. "A just resolution is one that focuses on repairing any harm to people and communities, achieving real accountability by making things right in so far as possible and bringing healing to all the parties."[6] Restorative justice principles and practices are consistent with previous disciplinary provisions, but the preference for these principles and practices has now been clearly affirmed. In 1996 the United Methodist Church adopted in its Social Principles restorative justice as the justice to be pursued in the criminal justice system.[7] In 2004 the delegates decided that any one going through the grievance procedure of the church, as well as those who are harmed, should be treated with the same justice.

There have been such processes, for example, for clergy who have stolen money. Here members of the local church are present who can talk about the harm to their community. The district superintendent and the chair of the Board of Ordained ministry are present to deal with the breach of the covenant of ministry. The minister and the minister's spouse are present along with their best friends to support them, but also to put the minister in context. Often an ex-offender is present, a minister who has stolen money and can help in dealing with harm and accountability as well as healing.

Healing is needed where sexual abuse has occurred. Mediators have questioned whether mediation is appropriate in such circumstances. Working together with Stephanie Hixon, I learned that circles can be appropriate places for such conversations. In circle, with the guidance of ritual, grounded in a relational covenant, and surrounded by supportive persons for all involved, we have experienced good things happen.

Conclusion

Is there any harm that cannot be dealt with at the Table, with the proper preparation, with the essential people being present, including those who help make it a relatively safe space, and with the agreement by all to the process?

What if church members participated in such restorative circles for first time offenders in our courts or for youth going through grievance procedures in our high schools? What if we as a church truly modeled restorative justice practices for the world?

The Table does not provide an easy fix. As Daniel Day Williams said, "Love does not resolve every conflict; it accepts conflict as the arena in which the word of love is to be done." The Table recognizes the arena of conflict and allows us to name it. The Table is about the work of Love.

Reflection Questions

1. What does the body of Christ or *ubuntu* mean to you and what are the implications for our life in community?

2. How might the lessons of conflict transformation help you deal with a conflict in your own life?

3. Describe lessons you have learned about dealing with conflicts and harm.

4. What ideas do you have for practice of reconcilliation at the Table?

Notes

1. I have not come to the conclusion that there was no place for the adversary system. There are cases that need to be tried, both because of important precedent setting issues, and because there will be cases where the parties are not able to resolve their disputes. In fact, there are some conflicts, especially those involving social injustices, which need to be heightened by strong advocates before right relations can be achieved.

2. Judith Herman, *Trauma and Recovery: The Aftermath of Violence—from Domestic Abuse to Political Terror*, (New York: Basic Books, 1992), 177.

3. Desmond Tutu, *No Future Without Forgiveness* (New York: Doubleday, 1999), p. 255.

4. Howard Zehr, *Changing Lenses: A New Focus for Crime and Justice* (Scottdale: Herald Press, 1990), 68.

5. Wheatley, Margaret, *Turning to One Another: Simple Conversations to Restore Hope to the Future* (San Francisco: Berrett-Koehler Publishers, Inc., 2002), 3.

6. *The Book of Discipline of the United Methodist Church* (Nashville: The United Methodist Publishing House, 2004), ¶ 362.

7. *The Book of Discipline of the United Methodist Church* (Nashville: The United Methodist Publishing House, 2004), ¶ 164H.

Chapter Eight

Holy Communion and the Healing of Relationships

Stephanie Anna Hixon

> *"We know that the whole creation has been groaning in labor pains until now; and not only the creation, but we ourselves . . . groan inwardly while we wait . . . For in hope we were saved . . . Likewise . . . that very Spirit intercedes with sighs too deep for words."* *(Rom 8:22-26)*

A Gift of Healing in Ordinary Time

It was a Sunday morning like so many others for this small community of faith. The children were arriving in the sanctuary from Sunday school, clutching the tangible project depicting today's lesson; the choir was hastily assembling for the late warm-up and prayer prior to worship; worshippers were finding their seats, extending greetings to familiar faces along the way; and the table was quietly being prepared by a member of the guild—bread, cup and freshly laundered linens.

As was their custom, members gathered in a circle around the table to eat and drink together, grounded in the gentle rhythm of this weekly celebration and nourishment.

"The body of Christ, given for you.."

"The blood of Christ, shed for you.."

"The body of .."

CRASH! BANG! ROLL! The offering plates on the side table fell to the floor as Harry[1] stumbled up the shallow steps to the table. On his knees, with concerned friends quickly surrounding him, it became apparent that Harry had been drinking. As friends helped him to his feet, communion was served, and among many stunned stares, Harry was escorted by friends to a room outside of the sanctuary.

A web of complex relationships was related to this experience—fractured, strained, and conflicted. There was that messy and confusing reality of how individuals and the community responded to this disruption of the familiar pattern around the Table of the Lord. Some were deeply troubled and offended. For Harry, it was the beginning of recovery and healing. He had been carrying the enormous burden of a secret for weeks. He had lost his job—an experience becoming all too common amid changes in the manufacturing industry in this area. As if the embarrassment and loss of dignity weren't painful enough, the family was facing mounting medical bills related to the birth and health of their third child. Harry experienced an odd sort of comfort in the numbed state of drinking alcohol.

Months passed before Harry entered that sanctuary again and stood in a circle of celebration of the presence of Christ at Table. As witnessed by Harry, in his own words to the congregation, there had been much hard work for him and his family during this time. Although their future as a family was uncertain, they were moving forward with help and support from caring professionals and from their friends in this community. He told the congregation that he knew there had been some gossip and hurt feelings about experiencing him under the influence of alcohol. Speculation about him and his family abounded. Generous acts of caring were extended including preparation of meals for the children and transportation to treatment. He asked them to respect the family's privacy and invited them to learn more about the nature of alcohol addiction and the challenges of caring for a child with terminal illness. He expressed gratitude for their caring. "The body of Christ, given for you . . . ." It was a signpost, a new mark of the journey toward healing for him, his family and this community. That seems to be the nature of healing for many.

> Healing is complex and takes place over time.
>
> Healing is often deeply personal and related to a larger community.
>
> Healing involves body, mind, spirit and relationships.
>
> Healing may include confronting difficult realities with truth.
>
> Healing is rooted and nourished in the fullness of a loving, compassionate and gracious God.

Being Mindful of Context: the Personal, Communal, and Systemic

How might the practice of Holy Communion offer courage and hope in the midst of conflicted and broken relationships? For Harry, Holy Communion was ritual and practice at the heart of the community to which he belonged. This deeply personal story is not unlike the stories many of us carry each time we come to the Table and receive the bread and cup. Part of Harry's personal journey became public due to the observed experience of his stumbling. The healing process involved contexts beyond the setting and ongoing practice of Holy Communion—interactions with family, congregational members, and caring professionals in the broader community. At an appropriate time in the healing process, Harry chose to offer his own witness. His participation with members of the congregation at Table marked a step in the journey toward healing and wholeness. And the journey toward wholeness did not stop at the Table: Harry acknowledged ongoing hard work. There were uneasy relationships with his family and the community of faith. What about the economic and social challenges that Harry and his family were facing? Was there support for families with ill and dying children? What was there to know about addictions and their impact on individuals, families, and communities? Were there inequities or injustices to be confronted?

Webs of relationships are connected with the soulful journeys of individuals, and these journeys unfold within specific contexts. Being mindful of context helps us to know one another and to be known more fully. Being mindful of context enables us to engage a healing process that addresses the many facets of conflicted and fractured relationships. Being mindful of those who are not at the Table and those who may stumble near the Table is a genuine response of faith. As people of faith, the practice of Holy Communion reminds us of the depth and nature of God's love and desire for communion with us, nourishes us in the depth and nature of that love, and compels us to live fully into the depth and nature of that love. As Marcia McFee notes in chapter six, Holy Communion becomes the ritual that forms and reshapes us. In that we can be encouraged and find hope.

For the Healing of the Nations

> For the healing of the nations, Lord we pray with one accord;
> for a just and equal sharing of the things that earth affords;
> (UMH #428)

Why focus on these systemic issues when considering Holy Communion and the healing of relationships? "Authentic reconciliation demands change in personal and systemic practices."[2] When relationships are conflicted and fractured, there may be systems of oppression, inequities, and injustices that contribute to conflict or perpetuate harm to individuals and communities of persons. The church is called to be an instrument of healing, justice, and peace in the world; striving faithfully for justice and peace is the context in which we may realize reconciliation and healing.

For me, it is important to be attentive to the world and creation at Table, to keep the community imagination alive and engaged in what it means to be the body of

Christ. Peacemakers must engage not only in ritual and practice such as mediation or circle processes, but also in activism that confronts the roots of injustice and oppression.[3]

That simple courageous act of Rosa Parks in Montgomery, Alabama in 1955 occurred in a context that extended beyond Ms. Parks' ride home from work. Her refusal to give up her seat on the bus to a white man was embedded in a network of activism in her community, not unlike other communities in the nation that subsequently galvanized around the U.S. civil rights movement. The Truth and Reconciliation Commission emerged in the ripeness of time amid a tumultuous battle against apartheid in South Africa. The anti-rape movement, naming rape as violence in the U.S., can be understood as an "attempt to carve out a moral stance against sexual violence."[4] The courage of survivors of sexual abuse to speak the truth about their experience began to break the silence. That was the context for education and awareness within religious settings about sexual abuse and misconduct by clergy and religious professionals. There are countless examples of advocacy and activism as faithful responses to God's call. What captures your imagination as a peacemaker or instrument for change in God's creation?

Restorative Processes, Healing, and Difficult Questions

What about those who have experienced seemingly unforgivable acts of violence or betrayal? Can and should those who have perpetrated harm and those who have been harmed come together at table? As one who has anguished over these difficult questions, I find it impossible to consider healing apart from justice. The principles of restorative justice are foundational (focus on harm; real accountability; and authentic engagement). In my faith journey, the capacity to venture toward healing with justice is formed and informed by Holy Communion. This Holy Mystery is where the now and the not yet meet. What I have come to know is the importance of being attentive to the questions, to engage the apparent tensions and contradictions, and to listen to those from whom and about whom difficult questions are asked.

I was not at all convinced that Julia should participate in this community meeting with Howard, a convicted sex offender who had raped her as a girl. Nearing the end of his prison term, Howard wished to return to the community where he had lived for fifty years. His elderly parents were members of the same congregation as Julia and her family. Julia, now an adult leader in the community, was insistent that this meeting was the only way to address the deep fears of having Howard present in the places of her life and work and her family's life and faith.

Although I knew that Howard had pursued an authentic path of accountability and transformation, this did not quell my anxiety about repeating patterns of abuse and potential for re-victimization. Nevertheless, I trusted Julia, and her determination of what would be most helpful. We considered together the "what if(s)?" related to such engagement. Julia explored the nature and details of the meeting with her support network and with local authorities. Her journey of healing and transformation had included hard grief and trauma work. She was confident that she wanted to name and negotiate her own terms of accountability and "co-existence" with Howard.

After much preparation, there was agreement about how the meeting would be conducted and who would be present—including support persons and officials related to the decision-making. The process involved a circle and took some time, but eventually all agreed to guidelines for interaction that included such things as education about the crime, transparency about the conviction, as well as the continued path of accountability. The circle established specific parameters regarding Howard's interaction with persons in the neighborhood and the congregation. For Julia, it was a powerful shift to be acting for what she wanted and needed rather than responding or reacting to others. These agreements were not entered into easily; and yet, they marked a moment of reconciliation. Changed relationships enabled persons to continue to move through transformation and experience healing.

In the practice of restorative processes, such as a circle, I am helped by John Paul Lederach's understanding of transformative peacemaking that upholds values often posed as an either/or contradiction:

> *Personal and systemic change* . . . the challenge of personal transformation . . . [and] equally involves the task and priority of systemic transformation, of increasing justice and equality in our world.

> *Micah's dilemma: the paradox of justice & mercy* . . . to . . . pursue justice in ways that respect people and to achieve restoration of relationships based on recognizing and amending injustices.

> *Empowerment and interdependence.* . . for . . . people to be involved in the decisions and environment that affect their lives.

> *Process and outcome.* . . . fair, respectful and inclusive process as a way of life and . . . outcome as a commitment to increasing justice, seeking truth, and healing relationships.[5]

Within church and community settings, a variety of processes may contribute to restoration and healing such as circle processes, facilitated conversations, mediation practices, victim/offender conferences, and/or community mediation. Circles hold promise for me because circles embrace paradox and complexity—they can resist the tendency to be defined by sides. Circles are flexible and adaptive according to the purpose for gathering (e.g., support, healing, accountability) and the needs and values of those who are gathered. As with any practice or process, circles can also be perilous. Not only is it important to be mindful of the integrity of circle processes, but these processes may also become captive to dominant paradigms serving those who benefit from preserving the status quo.

Jennifer was a bit uneasy about being face to face with Pastor Ray. Although she had a support person with her, no one had informed her about what to expect.

She felt overwhelmed in this circle of church leaders and was eager put this horrible experience of betrayal by Pastor Ray behind her. Everyone seemed relieved when the decisions were made. At the end of the process, the person facilitating the circle invited everyone to stand, hold hands and sing "Blest Be the Tie That Binds." That moment was like a blow to her stomach; she felt the breath sucked out of her. She wondered why it seemed so important to some that everyone appear to be in unity. She knew that the facilitator was well meaning. She was fine with respect for one another and for God in a decision-making process; however, holding hands and singing about the "tie that binds" seemed forced and artificial to her.

Consider the Process

I find the contributions of Kay Pranis and colleagues a helpful place from which to reflect on the nature and purpose of circle processes when considering situations where harm has been perpetrated against another. I am reminded that ". . . the circle process is by nature messy, because humans and their conflicts are messy. Moreover, each process is different, because each case is unique."[6] Circles (people coming together for a specific purpose) can be used at each stage of the process. Exploration of the following stages of circle process for dealing with crime by Pranis, et al., provides a framework for considering potential promise and peril of circle processes. The stages are not necessarily linear.

> *Stage 1. Determining suitability*: Is the circle the best process to use?
>
> *Stage 2. Preparation*: What preparation do the different parties need before they come together? Extensive preparation may be required for participants when there has been betrayal or harm.
>
> *Stage 3. The Circle*: What process best meets the needs of everyone involved? When parties . . . come together to decide how to repair harm, what process can meet the needs of everyone involved? This stage develops a consensus—an agreement.
>
> *Stage 4. Follow-up and maintaining accountability*: What happens next? Is arriving at an agreement the end as it is in the courts, or is it a new beginning? How are agreements carried out, and what happens if someone breaks an agreement? There may be review circles in this stage.[7]

Because of the adaptability of circle processes, Pranis, Stuart, and Wedge offer guidance about when circle processes may *not* be appropriate:

> *Lack of balance* . . . If a potential circle lacks balanced representation, and if the Circle community has not been through a training to develop skills, it isn't wise to proceed.
>
> *Lack of time* . . . How much time is needed depends on the peo-

ple involved. Staging a Circle . . . without the resolve to continue can be harmful to everyone.

Capacity . . . Are the resources available to do a Circle? [e.g., trained circle keepers and those who can see a process through all four stages.] Although Circles can deal with offenses such as sexual assault and spousal abuse, it's critical that appropriate resources for professional input and treatment are available. In such cases, victims' advocates need to be involved from beginning to end.

Safety . . . issues of safety [for participants] and the danger of revictimizing victims may require a different choice of process . . . an alternative may be to design one Circle for the victim and another for the offender.

Urgency . . . Circles can't guarantee a solution by a set date or time.[8]

Tom Porter wrote about the possibility of circle processes for dealing with harm, accountability, and healing related to situations of sexual abuse perpetrated by leaders in the Church. For me, it seems potentially perilous to suggest suitability of circles and other restorative practices in these situations; however, I have been witness to the promise and power of healing when circles have gathered for the purpose of seeking just resolution. "A just resolution is one that focuses on repairing any harm to people and communities, achieving real accountability by making things right in so far as possible and bringing healing to all the parties."[9] I have also witnessed restorative processes such as healing circles for survivors of abuse or healing circles within congregations that occurred alongside or subsequent to other processes for adjudication.

Candace Benyei provides some insights specific to clergy misconduct based on family systems theory. She writes, "Congregations have participated in keeping the secret . . . . In order to protect cherished illusions of the clergyperson as parent/protector of the family, congregants have scapegoated the truth-tellers and deeply damaged their families of faith . . . . While loyalty is a survival resource for the community as a whole, it can also cause the family of faith to tolerate abuse of individuals in the service of the system."[10]

Truth-telling and acknowledgment of harm are significant parts of healing for most, given the secrecy that often surrounds abuse. Whether considering issues of safety, the importance of advocates and support persons, clarity of purpose about a process, or genuine involvement of participants in determining the nature of engagement, preparation is critical.

Nancy Myer Hopkins, a family therapist and consultant in matters related to clergy sexual misconduct within church settings states, "Mediation should never be attempted before a thorough investigation, and is most effective if any discipline of the offender has already been determined. Religious leaders should understand that a good mediator is well trained and highly skilled. Furthermore, successful mediation requires much advance preparation by both parties before a meeting to ensure there is a reasonable chance of a positive outcome, and that a victim-survivor will not be revictimized in the process."[11]

I have real fears about church leaders approaching holy communion and restorative processes as a utilitarian means to an end.   If I draw from my experience with survivors of sexual abuse by religious professionals, I am reminded that for many, the sacred signs and symbols of faith have been misused in order to perpetrate abuse.   Experiencing them anew as sacred and meaningful can take a long time; this often involves a different community within a context of safety. I am mindful of the call and responsibility to be stewards of these holy mysteries.

I have seen how restorative processes have been reshaped by and for survivors in ways that honor their sacred stories.   Most adjudication (particularly in a retributive model) places the person who has experienced harm at a distance to the process and their narrative—their story.   Their narrative is often repeated, examined, prodded, challenged, and torn apart to try to determine verity.   There is power and restoration in choosing how to participate in a process, determining what of one's story is shared, telling one's own truth, and contributing to decisions about accountability and healing.

Most powerfully, I can bear witness to the wonder of persons being known in context and the genuineness that is fostered when persons are able to enter in good faith, agree to the nature and purpose of a circle, acknowledge the presence of the sacred in the process and one another.   I have had the sacred privilege of being with persons in deeply anguishing moments of bitterness, pain, tears, laughter, disbelief, and genuine struggle to acknowledge truth and harm, and to choose transformation and healing. I have witnessed the creative engagement of imagination as circle participants seek just agreement about paths of healing, accountability and restoration. For some, it is the act of acknowledgment of harm, a commitment to a journey of repentance and authentic steps toward accountability, even sharing signs of forgiveness that free persons from burdens of the memories of harm and open new paths for healing.

Forgiveness, Being Reconciled, Called to be Reconcilers

What about forgiveness being, as Marjorie Thompson has described, a "ticklish" subject? Forgiveness "involves an entire disposition of mind, heart, and will. [And that] . . . forgiving is not necessarily forgetting although we can learn to recall the hurt in a different light."[12] Indeed, for many survivors of violence, abuse or harm, the burden of memory shifts in the process of forgiveness. "No one should be asked to forgive an abuser."[13] Citing the words of Carol J. Adams that, 'Forgiveness in the absence of repentance by the abuser is a salve for the conscience of society, but it is not a healing experience for the victim.'[14] K. Louise Schmidt adds, ". . . neither is it healing for the perpetrator, for it prevents the necessary steps of transformation and healing to take place for both."[15]

For John, Judith, and Suzanne, the circle of healing they experienced with members of the congregation where they had been targets of abuse by a religious professional was an opportunity to mourn what was lost in their faith and relationships in that community. Their lives would never be the same, nor would the life of the congregation. The healing circle marked a moment of reconciliation in the journey toward wholeness.

For the families of Brandon and Thomas, rocked by the deadly gang violence that stole their sons' lives, the circle of healing hosted by the congregation was a safe place to begin to rebuild lives and relationships in the community.

For Harry, stumbling to the altar led to standing anew at the Table—a moment of healing on his journey toward wholeness.

For one South African mother during the Truth and Reconciliation Commission who declared that she would be the mother of her son's murderer, there was a moment of reconciliation in the journey toward justice and healing. Her son's memory would not be forgotten; she entered a new relationship with another son. Their lives were inextricably woven together in this redemptive journey.

I am encouraged by the wisdom shared by Peter Storey:

> We come with little other than good faith. We need to be very careful that we don't put too much trust, in our "skills" as if they are weapons, our version of armaments. It is our empty-handedness that may help us to be useful to the cause of peacebuilding.
> . . .
>
> It is going to be very costly to go on loving. We need to go from the Table committed to each other, in covenant to pray for one another, resource one another, listen to one another, be in silence with one another, celebrate with one another, hold one another accountable and act with one another for peace.[16]

In community we glimpse the wonder and despair of relationships intertwined with one another and with God. In the practice of Holy Communion, we open ourselves to the living and healing presence of God and to the imaginative possibilities of the fullness of God's restoration and *shalom*.

Reflection Questions

1. Consider Harry's story. Does Harry's story open new questions or insights for you about Holy Communion, healing, and relationships?

2. As you reflect on the examples of activism as part of reconciliation and heal-

ing, what captures your imagination as a peacemaker or instrument for change in God's creation?

3. What are some of the difficult questions for you when considering the possibility of Holy Communion and the healing of relationships?

4. Are there situations that you feel are seemingly unforgivable—perhaps even beyond the potential for healing and reconciliation? What do you find most hopeful—most promising as you reflect on Holy Communion, healing, and justice?

Notes

1. I am grateful to those who have agreed to share their stories through this chapter. To honor confidentiality and respect the privacy of persons, names, and specific circumstances have been altered.

2. Gayle Carlton Felton, See Chapter 2.

3. For a fuller discussion of this "long view" of conflict and the nature of peacemaking, see the works of John Paul Lederech, noted teacher and international conflict transformation specialist.

4. Marie Fortune, "Why we do what we do . . . working to end sexual and domestic violence," (FaithTrust Institute Speech, October 25, 2003). Available at www.faithtrustinstitute.org.

5. John Paul Lederach. *Preparing for Peace: Conflict Transformation Across Cultures* (Syracuse: Syracuse University Press, 1995), 19-23.

6. Kay Pranis, Barry Stuart, and Mark Wedge, *Peacemaking Circles: From Crime to Community* (St. Paul: Living Justice Press, 2003), 152-153.

7. Ibid., 153.

8. Ibid.,157-158.

9. *The Book of Discipline of the United Methodist Church* (Nashville: The United Methodist Publishing House, 2004), ¶ 362.

10. Candace R. Benyei, *Understanding Clergy Misconduct in Religious Systems: Scapegoating, Family Secrets, and the Abuse of Power* (Binghamton: Haworth Press, 1998), xiii, 19.

11. Nancy Myer Hopkins, "The Uses and Limitations of Various Models for Understanding Clergy Sexual Misconduct: The Impact on the Congregation," *Journal of Sex Education and Therapy* 24 (4) (1999): 272.

12. Marjorie Thompson, Chapter 4.

13. K. Louise Schmidt, *Transforming Abuse: Nonviolent Resistance and Recovery* (Philadelphia: New Society Publishers, 1995), 134.

14. Emilie Buchwald, Pamela Fletcher, and Martha Roth, eds., *Transforming a Rape Culture* (Minneapolis: Milkweed Editions, 1994), 77.

15. Ibid.

16. Peter Storey, Chapter 5.

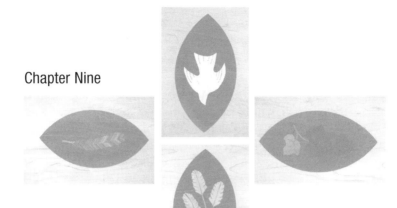

Chapter Nine

Grandma's Supper Is the Lord's Supper
The Experience of African American Fellowship Meals and Sunday Supper as Communion

David Anderson Hooker

> *Every time a gathering of people, under the protection of Spirit, triggers a body of emotional energy aimed at bringing them very tightly together, a ritual of one type or another is in effect . . . . There are two parts to ritual. One part is planned: people prepare the space for the ritual and think through the general choreography of the process. The other part of ritual cannot be planned because it is the part that the Spirit is in charge of. . . .Because ritual is so deeply connected to our human nature, any time it is missing there will be a lack of transformation and healing*[1]

I was raised in a Progressive Baptist tradition, which practiced believer's Baptism. Until I had joined the church and was baptized, I was not allowed to participate in the actual Service of Holy Communion. I was, however, always allowed to participate in the fellowship meal and in the "family"[2] dinners at my grandparents' house. Like most Christians (either consciously or not), my Christian hermeneutic was formed at that table. Long before I was old enough to study or learn the Bible lessons about Jesus' birth, death, and resurrection, I heard the stories of the power of the Holy Spirit and God's saving grace and the friendship of Jesus. I also learned what was required of me in terms of my community: do justice—do what's right; love mercy—welcome and protect the orphan and the stranger, love those who love you and those who do not; and walk humbly—speak truth to power in love. The stories told by my elders, kin, and community shaped the perspective I adopted when I would later study the actual Scriptures, teaching, and doctrine of the church.

When I entered seminary more than a quarter century after my first communion, we were tasked with writing a description of our first communion. My Catholic, Anglican, and Episcopal colleagues recalled their communion coming on the heels of confirmation. Others recalled communion as occurring shortly after their baptism. For me, my first experience of communion was at my grandmother's[3] dinner table. My mother is the eldest of nine children raised by two dedicated parents in Moultrie, Georgia. My mother and most of her siblings moved away from Moultrie soon after they graduated high school. They left either to attend college or to start a life in a context other than the segregated Deep South. Like my mother, most of her siblings sought to maintain an intergenerational connection to their birthplace and so they sent their children back to Moultrie every summer to spend time with grandparents and among cousins.

Every Sunday my siblings and I attended church. Every Sunday after church we, like seemingly every other family in the community, had family dinner at my grandparents' home. On the first Sunday of the month, all the families served a combined dinner, which was held in the church fellowship hall before the Sunday night communion service. Each week, as the family meal or fellowship dinner was winding down talk would take an inevitable turn to the "prayers of the people." Someone would begin to tell a story of a current personal or communal struggle, dilemma, or triumph. In response, either as validation, encouragement or in search of solutions, others would tell personal stories or the stories of our fore parents and ancestors. All of the stories were relayed in relationship to biblical stories or as a parable expressing a belief about the role of God in attaining vindication, salvation or strength for the journey. The values and virtues conveyed were usually confirmed by a scriptural text (I once was young and now I am old and I have *never* seen the righteous forsaken . . .) or one of the wisdom sayings of an elder ("granddaddy always said . . . ").

While the sacramental acts of baptism or confirmation (depending on your tradition) serve as your *individual* induction into the household of faith, the sacrament of the Lord's Supper is the church's central act of *community* formation. Similarly, while your birth or marriage into a family may be heralded, the central act of community formation in African American communities is the Sunday family dinner. Participation clearly marks you as a member of the community with the privileges and responsibilities entailed therein.

My first experience of communion was not in a church per se nor did it occur during the sacramental ceremony prescribed by the doctrine of the church. Rather, I first participated in communion at my grandmother's table on a summer Sunday afternoon and in the fellowship hall of the church. It was not presented to me as communion and, yet, I now recognize that all the elements of a Eucharist celebration were present. My experience was neither singular nor rare in African American communities and, I suspect, it was not unique to African American communities. Certain activities seem universal in their capacity to unite people, to overcome political, economic, social, and other barriers created by our constructed identities and to forge reconciliation when that becomes necessary. Eating, music, and story-telling are chief among these activities.

This chapter offers a vision of the African/African American fellowship meal as the site for celebration of Holy Communion. My vision is not of symbolic communion or as a model celebration. Rather, I am describing the Sunday fellowship meal as the actual celebration of communion. While I am certain that each community has a meal/event that could serve this capacity, I am familiar with the African/African American community fellowship meal. I am also aware that there are certain dynamics of eating and table fellowship unique to African Americans that could be incorporated into the meal/communion service.

I will first consider the development of the Black Church and how the "family dinner"/ fellowship meal became closely linked with celebration of communion. I will then consider aspects of the sacrament ritual. I will also describe the way in which this same table fellowship practice could bridge the racial/economic/political divide and allow us to reclaim the true spirit of table fellowship that Jesus inaugurated and invited us into. This is not research; this is a vision.

The Black Church, The Fellowship Meal, and Holy Communion

As one aspect of the systemic degradation that occurred during the enslavement era in the U.S., the enslavers made every effort to strip enslaved Africans of their culture. The imposed structures were economic, political, linguistic, and religious. The enslavers made stringent efforts to separate family members and destroy the possibilities for communal and familial bonding. Equal effort was put into destruction of spoken languages and religious practice. Euro-Western Christianity was offered as a substitute religious format and all aspects of Traditional African Religious practices were forbidden, even outlawed. In order to outlaw these practices, most rituals and all forms of sacrifice were halted. Historically, at least in the U.S. the fellowship meal became closely associated with the celebration of communion as a creative response to the hegemonic constraints of slave era religiosity.

During this period in plantation economies, because most clergy were itinerant, the celebration of communion happened infrequently (quarterly, semi-annually, and in some instances once a year or even less). Many historical records of that period suggest that those enslaved persons that participated in the observation of Holy Communion were brought together with the enslaved of other plantation systems in a regional celebration. After the celebration of Holy Communion, most often there was a period in which the enslaved Africans would socialize among themselves and have a large shared fellowship meal. Often husbands and wives, parents and children, kindred and homefolks were only able to re-connect with one another during these post-communion fellowship meals. In this way, this fellowship meal became the defining act of community (re)formation—the times in which the stories or triumph and trial were shared; the times in which encouragement and uplift were offered and the times in which liberation strategies were authored and communicated. This was the time where the enslaved African could actually envision the heavenly banquet with a modicum of freedom and a table where they could come without degradation (at least momentary). It was in these moments that they could truly experience Jesus' invitation to the heavenly banquet.

Grandma's Supper Is the Lord's Supper

Other than my very first church-based communion, my experience with the Holy Communion ceremony offered by the church was subsequently less profound, less relevant and ultimately less formational in my faith than were my communion experiences at my grandmother's table and those in the fellowship hall. Having now studied the dimensions of the Holy Rite, there are many reasons why I experience the fellowship meal as the actual communion. Among these are:

1. Family Dinner as site for the celebration of Holy Communion reclaims the celebratory dimensions of the original experience. Holy Communion has both a spiritual dimension and a worldly dimension. Communion is the representation of the heavenly feast or kingdom banquet. It is also the time in which two reconciling acts occur: those between God and humanity, and between humanity and humanity. In modern celebrations most denominations retain a solemn and somber atmosphere for the observation of Eucharist. The synoptic Gospels each record that Jesus wished to celebrate Passover with the disciples before he was to be handed over to the authorities to suffer. Passover recalls the difficult times of bondage and enslavement that Israel had experienced. However, there is also a reason for celebration. In his classic exploration of faith in community, *Life Together*, Dietrich Bonhoeffer wrote:

> The fellowship of the table has a festive quality. It is a constantly recurring reminder in the midst of our everyday work of God's resting after His work, of the Sabbath as the meaning and goal of the week and its toil. . . . Through *our daily meals* He is calling us to rejoice, to keep holiday in the midst of our working day.[4] (italics added)

In addition to noting the celebratory quality of table fellowship, Bonhoeffer also suggests that the table fellowship in which we celebrate God's acts of redemption and salvation should be our everyday meal experience and not necessarily a time set apart from our ordinary existence.

The Dictionary of Biblical Imagery observes that: "[f]easts in the Bible are images of joyful voices, festive music, dancing and abundant food. They are not simply parties, but celebrations of God's goodness toward [God's] people. Feasts provide occasions for fellowship with one another and with the Lord to remember and celebrate what wonderful things God has done."[5] Banquets and feasts are often seen and experienced as a foretaste of God's heavenly banquet. "The Eucharist is the feast of the whole church as it participates in and yet awaits the perfect reign of God. And what we expect to become, we seek to be now."[6]

2. Reclaiming the tradition of orality. Family and fellowship dinners are a more accessible occasion to recall the pain and triumph of personal history and connect our human story to the divine story in the midst of community celebration. These are also excellent occasions to connect the past and present to the hopes of the future. Before the Gospels were preserved in writing, the stories and the power of the stories of Jesus were kept alive in the Afro-Asiatic oral tradition of first century Palestine. In Christian Scriptures, the first written account of the Eucharist is in Paul's letter to the church at Corinth: "For I received from the Lord what I also handed on to you . . . ." This indicates that the tradition is primarily an oral tradition and not initially a written one. Paul referred to what he received in the apostolic tradition.

The current celebration of the Eucharist in the context of liturgy is generally formulaic and repeated from one celebration to the next. Placed in the context of the family/fellowship meal, the Lord's Supper has a greater chance of reclaiming the tradition of orality that first preserved the traditions linking the daily-lived stories of Christian community with the divine stories and the Biblical record. Emmanuel McCarthy observes: "the Eucharist, like the Gospels, originates in a predominantly oral culture. Therefore the memory or remembrance that the original Apostolic tradition would have been preserving, narrating and passing on would have been an oral memory."[7]

Attempting to contain all the expressions of thanksgiving and the narrative history of the saving and redeeming acts of God in a written liturgical format constrains the Holy Spirit and distances the act of Eucharistic thanksgiving from the people and from their daily lived experience. It fails to link the life story with the Biblical story or to connect the human story to the divine story.

Anne Streaty Wimberly notes "[s]tory linking is a process whereby we connect parts of our everyday stories with the Christian faith story in the Bible and the exemplars of the Christian faith outside the Bible . . . . The story-linking process can help us open ourselves to God's call to act in ways that are liberating for us and others and to decide how we will do this"[8] The purpose of the story-linking process allows us to see biblical history through our personal and communal lived experience and to see our personal and communal lived experience through the Biblical story. The central story of Christian life is the Passion and resurrection of the Christ. This story is bounded by two occasions in which Jesus breaks bread with some or all of his disciples (Holy Thursday and Emmaus Road). Centering the experience of community formation around and viewing community formation through the lens of these stories, serves to deepen the experience of Emmanuel—God with us.

Linking the Jesus story with the stories of Christian disciples and martyrs adds potency to the lived experience and relevance of the stories. A story becomes even more knowable and particular when biblical personalities and historical legends are connected with the personal legends and ancestors of the family gathered at the table for fellowship. When I hear the stories of the exploits of General George Washington Monroe Gaines Hill—my maternal great grandfather—I feel that God has been active through the ages in not only my life but the life of my entire family.

3. The Eucharist is the meal of the church, which represents the coming feast or heavenly banquet and connects the past present and future of God's reign. Because the Eucharist is a meal of the church, embedded in any theology of the sacrament is an ecclesiology—a set of assumptions about the nature of the church.[9] A Eucharistic liturgy that is primarily focused on the individual benefits of the reception of the sacrament leads to individualistic notions of salvation and the church as a source of individual healing and wholeness. The genius of the Reformation is that Martin Luther, by translating the Bible into German, began the process of liberating the Gospel from its captivity to Rome and allowed it to be rooted in other cultures. Situating the experience of Holy Communion in the Sunday family/fellowship dinner of African Americans continues the Reformation. While a European worldview informs an individualistic Christianity that promotes individualistic conversion as the method of attaining salvation, African (and most indigenous) world viewing understands that our existence occurs only in community—"I am because you are and because you are therefore I am."

The theology of sacrament detailed in the African American fellowship meal emphasizes the collective nature of the struggle and the present actors' continuing role as a member of a community. The theology of the fellowship meal is collective and the hermeneutic is often one of struggle, faith in the struggle, the accompaniment of Jesus, and the power of the Holy Spirit. By telling the stories of the faithful, we remind everyone present at the table that the invitation to the feast is open to all and yet, there is an expectation that those who participate are making a commitment to the continued work of bringing God's realm into full manifestation in this present age.

"Heaven is not only about the future, but it is also about the past and the present. It is a means of connecting Christians now alive with all who went before them. Whatever else eternal life is, it is the "communion of the saints"—the bond of grace between all Christians living and dead. The loss of the concept of heaven is also the loss of a companionship we rightly feel with those who have preceded us in the faith."[10] To gather at the Lord's Table and to be joined by "the saints and all the company of heaven" is also characterized in African tradition as the joining of the ancestors and those that preceded us both in the faith *and in the struggle.*

Further, the family/fellowship meal is the appropriate venue for celebrating Holy Communion because the community is not bound by textual constraints. Rather, it is free to interpret the text and contextualize the appropriate form of remembrance and celebration. In *Springtime of the Liturgy*[11], in commenting on the study of "the Eucharistic liturgy," Lucien Diess notes that:

> The community is bent on celebrating the Eucharist rather than on describing it in writing; *it lives the Eucharist and only secondarily turns to analyzing the structure of the celebration.* The community is first, not the text, while the text is entirely in the service of the community.[12]

4. The family dinner/fellowship meal has more ritual and less ceremony; more ritual and less ceremony provides a place for the Holy Spirit. Malidoma Patrice Somé in his seminal work, *The Healing Wisdom of Africa* distinguishes between "ritual" and "ceremony" in this way: Ceremony is planned, orchestrated, and does not have a spontaneous element; therefore, it lacks the presence and action of the Spirit. Ritual, on the other hand, is bound by sacred space and symbols and is planned or conceived to the extent that the intentionality and purpose are specified; after this point then Spirit is invoked and its presence is given reign over the place and participants to accomplish the intended purpose.[13] Rituals assist communities in their formation, stabilization, strengthening, strategizing and the search for hope

Holy Communion is currently observed in most settings as, in Somé's terminology, more ceremony than ritual. Small, flat wafers symbolize bread and a thimble-full (or less) of pasteurized grape juice symbolizes wine. The symbols—bread and wine—are themselves symbols of body and blood; which are symbols of a new covenant. To take one step further back and symbolize the symbols through elements (bread and juice) in a form not experienced in the daily lived experience of the partakers and to attempt to capture the experience in a written and formulaic presentation creates every opportunity for disengagement and detachment from the experience. This severe detachment makes it more difficult to link the divine story of Jesus' nonviolent, unconditional love of friends and enemies to our every day lived experiences in ways that allow us to have a "remembrance" of Jesus and/or to recognize our risen Lord in the faces of the other with whom we share a place at the table.

In each of the synoptic gospels the last supper, the Lord's Supper, takes place within the context of a full meal. The meal is associated with Passover or the Feast of Unleavened Bread. In both of these feasts, Israel remembers in great detail how God delivered them from the grip of oppressive forces and restored them from exile. They also remember how they were chastised and taken into exile for forgetting the ordinances of the Lord. Beyond the Last Supper, there are many other occasions where Scripture recounts Jesus enjoying table fellowship with disciples and also with sinners and otherwise marginalized persons (Matt 9:11; Mark 2:16; Luke 5:30,

7:36-50, 19:1-10). In each instance there is room for the Spirit to enter the sacred space and direct the experience.

5. As often as you do this, do this in remembrance of me. Do this. When Jesus gave instruction regarding the act that has become the celebration of the Eucharist—whenever you do this, do so in remembrance of me—he was probably not speaking about sharing a Passover meal or some ritual gathering. More likely, he spoke of the every day acts of breaking bread and sharing bread and wine as a collective. This interpretation is furthered by the Emmaus Road experience in which the disciples sharing an evening meal with Jesus "recognized him in the breaking of the bread." Emmaus Road was not a particularly festive time or a time associated with a large community gathering. Rather, it occurred in the occasional meal that accompanies the return after a long journey or the evening meal at the end of a day. The fellowship meal, while most often occurring on Sunday can indeed happen spontaneously and at other intervals not associated with a synchronized assembly.

In remembrance of me. The term used and translated as "remembrance," is *anamnesis.* There would have been a different understanding of that term than would be implied in modern translations. Modern translations render this word "remember." While we think of remembrances as thoughts and recollections, what was intended by Paul, and what would have been understood by Paul's audience, was the idea of remembrance as doing or recreating an event, or as an active even ritual repetition of an action. The *anamnesis* also suggests that the purpose of the action was to allow Jesus to be included in the fellowship.

ARGUMENTS AGAINST THIS IDEA

Many arguments stand against this proposal. Each of them can be met and still retain the sacramental experience of the Eucharist. I am not suggesting replacing one form of celebration with the other. I am suggesting that there be a variety of venues, services, and formats in which we could celebrate the Holy Communion, thereby increasing the presence in our daily lives.

Laurence Stookey argues that when celebrating Eucharist:

> 1. The Eucharist is congregational and this should be held as "the norm."

> 2. The rite has (and should retain) specific elements. Those elements should closely resemble those detailed by Hippolytus (circa 215 A.D.)(Opening, Institution, Anamnesis, Epiclesis, Eucharistic Prayer, Doxology)

> 3. The rite has (and should retain) its four-fold action (Take, Break, Give thanks, Share)

> The actual communion elements should not be varied significantly from current practice.

4. Furnishings [should resemble a table but be higher because no one sits there].

5. Eucharist should be preserved only for the baptized.[14]

While each of these concerns argues against my proposal, I do not believe that any one of them cannot be overcome if our intention is to expand the experience of table fellowship and deepen its place in our lives. The family and house church was the first form of congregation. A liturgical format could be established to include six specific elements of the rite, maintain the four-fold action and incorporate the breaking of actual bread and the consumption of wine (or the appropriate substitute) without de-solemnizing the experience. Regarding the furniture for celebration, it is not at all clear why Stookey believes that the table should not allow persons to recline or at least sit. Certainly at the time of the institution of the sacrament the practice was to sit and recline (one disciple is identified as the one who "reclined next to Jesus.") And there are certainly doctrinal disagreements as to the openness of the table for purposes of fellowship. In addition to Stookey's arguments, other arguments have been raised for my consideration.

Holy Communion is holy and the space in which it is celebrated should only be sacred space. This argument reflects the very European/dualistic notion and understanding of the world. African and indigenous world viewings do not distinguish between sacred and profane or secular space. All space is sacred if we claim it as sacred. The space could be marked out and claimed as sacred by the pouring of libations, lighting of candles, or some other ritual act that demarks the space as sacred in that moment.

The purpose of the Eucharist is to celebrate a specific event in the life of the Church. Family meals are not "special" enough to maintain the significance of the celebration. How do you keep the meal from devolving to just an ordinary experience? At every stage of life: birth, naming, puberty, significant educational/developmental periods, adulthood, marriage, and death, we celebrate, restructure our community in light of the new occurrences and mark the significance of the event with a meal. It is possible that celebrating the Eucharist within a more familiar format of a family meal will lesson the significance of the celebration. It is equally possible that the celebration would increase in its relation to our everyday lived experience. The impact will reflect our individual intentions.

If everyone is welcome to celebrate at the table, then we are no longer celebrating the church. An exclusive celebration of the Lord's Supper seems to be the opposite of the table fellowship that Jesus practiced in his earthly ministry. In my family, we have individuals and entire branches of the family that adhere to a different set of creeds and beliefs (Seventh Day Adventists, Jehovah's Witnesses, Buddhists, Ba`hai, and agnostic as well as Methodist, Baptist, and members of the United Church of Christ). One of the primary reasons that people in my family chose to not share table fellowship together is because of the different creedal commitments. But I recall Jesus speaking with a Samaritan woman at the well. The woman reminded him that she and he (a Samaritan and a Jew) were divided about many things, not the least of which was creed and religious practice—"Our ancestors worshiped on this mountain, but you say that the place where people must worship is in Jerusalem."

And Jesus explained to her:

> Woman, believe me, the hour is coming when you will worship the Father neither on this mountain nor in Jerusalem. You worship what you do not know; we worship what we know, for salvation is from the Jews. But the hour is coming, and is now here, when the true worshipers will worship the Father in spirit and truth, for the Father seeks such as these to worship him. God is spirit, and those who worship him must worship in spirit and truth. (John 4:20-26)

Jesus was a friend of the marginalized, despised, and outcast. The authorities of that day often grumbled and complained that he had table fellowship with sinners and tax collectors (and women). (Matt 11:19; Luke 15:1-2) It would seem counter intuitive and antagonistic to the notion of discipleship if Jesus urged us to engage in table fellowship only among those who already believed in him. The offering of salvation embodied in the celebration of Communion is a gift freely given and not something that we can merit or earn. Exclusion of others is not within the scope of *our* decision-making authority.

What do we eat? The Eucharist is only the bread and wine as symbolic of the body and blood of Jesus. The original celebration occurred within the context of an entire meal and I argue the context should be restored closer to its original setting. Unleavened bread eaten at Passover recalls a time when the move of God was so fast that the Jews were taken out of Egypt without having had time to allow the bread to rise. Similarly, certain traditional dishes (e.g. chitlins, greens cooked with fatback, cornbread) recall a time in the life of many African/African American families when the food that was available was the discard of the plantation masters and the crops that could be secretly produced outside the control of the plantation owners/managers. This is almost the equivalent of African American manna.

For the meal to be experienced *as* communion, a specific intentionality must be expressed. Every time family is at the table, the role of the celebrant operates outside of what has become the traditional celebration of the Lord's supper. The rewards for doing so are (1) the revitalization of the traditional African spirit of worship; (2) the permeation of the Spirit into all aspects of life; and (3) the development of a more intentionally sacramental life.

Dimensions of the Meal that Resemble the Heavenly Banquet

Finally, I would recount certain aspects of the fellowship meal experience at my grandmother's table that offered me a foretaste of the heavenly banquet.

Everyone's presence is desired and expected. When my grandmother announced dinner, there was an expectation of full participation and the table was set in anticipation of everyone attending. It seems that when the final banquet is convened in God's realm, there is an expectation that everyone will be present and the table is set with room for all.

There is room at the table and there is plenty for all. This speaks to the abundance of God's provision now and in the realm to come. My grandmother began each meal after the prayer with the same refrain: "What you see, you are welcome to; what you don't see, don't ask." In some way this speaks to the experience of abundance that does not cross the line to gluttony and greed. The table is set and there is plenty for all. Be content with what's available; do not covet what you think others may have. There was another aspect of abundance reflected in the calling to the table. Sometime when children from the community knew that there was not enough food at their home they would invite themselves to stay for dinner. This had the potential of creating an embarrassing situation for the parents of those children. My grandmother would always ask, "Where is your mother?" If the child said, "At home," then my grandmother would ask one of the adults to call the parents and ask the parents and other siblings to come to dinner, "and tell them they're late and we're waiting!!" Their presence was welcome, expected, and celebrated.

Each person is equally valued and their individual gifts are celebrated. Because of space constraints, there were several tables set for dinner. Usually, the children sat at one table, the youth and young adults sat at another and the elders sat at "the big table." This did not reflect a bias or a diminished value of any of the participants at dinner. As I graduated to the "big table" I learned that much of the talk was about the pride and hope that was represented by those seated at the kids' table. There were members of our family that adopted different faith practices (Jehovah's Witnesses, Seventh Day Adventists, and Buddhists). Knowing that this caused some tension in the family, they were often hesitant to come to Sunday dinner. Even when she was sure they might refuse, Grandma Pauline always made sure someone called them to tell them when we were having dinner and what they could bring. Their presence was desired, their gifts were celebrated, and the meal was not complete without them. Table fellowship is incomplete if only those that agree with us are present at the table!

Conflicts are reconciled or resolved in order to come to the table. The disagreements that were present between siblings were usually addressed in the gathering process knowing that we would all sit at the table together. Reconciled community is the expectation at the family table in contrast to the current practices of our churches and denominations, where schism and division are open, acceptable and sometimes, encouraged points of conversation.

Conclusion

At the end of the day, the Eucharist is a celebration of table fellowship which foretells of the lavish welcome that God has prepared for us as a beloved community.

The bread and the wine are our soul's food. The best venue in which to feed our soul is at the Sunday dinner fellowship table as constructed in the African American experience. Abundance, extravagant welcome, equality, reconciliation, and the process of linking our individual and community stories to the divine story as recorded in Scripture and recalled by our ancestors and fore-parents through the ages. The proposed change is not just for African Americans: it is for all of God's children.

Reflection Questions

1. In what ways are your community/family fellowship meals like a communion? And how are they different?

2. What theology is on display during these gatherings?

3. Describe a time when your lived experience was connected through story to the biblical experience.

Notes

1. Malidoma Patrice Somé, *The Healing Wisdom of Africa* (New York: Tarcher/Putnam, 1998), 142, 145.

2. I use the term "family" very loosely because there was an extended circle and permeable boundary drawn around those that made up my "family/community." Indeed, I was fully adult before I realized that many of my "auntees," "uncles," and "cousins" had no blood relationship with me or anyone else who attended the "family" dinners.

3. My reference to "grand*mother*'s table" is intended to reflect the gender specified domains of authority that existed in the African American (and I suspect most other) communities during the time of my childhood.

4. Dietrich Bonhoeffer, *Life Together: The Classic Exploration of Faith in Community*, (New York: Harper and Row Publishers, Inc., 1954), 68.

5. Leland Ryken, James C. Wilhoit, and Tremper Longman III, eds., *Dictionary of Biblical Imagery* (Downers Grove: InterVarsity Press, 1998).

6. Luarence Hull Stookey, *Eucharist: Christ's Feast With the Church* (Nashville: Abingdon Press, 1993), 26.

7. Emmanuel Charles McCarthy, "A Scholarly Approach: Do This in Remembrance of Me" (centerforchristiannonviolence.org), 13.

8. Wimberly, Ann 39

9. Stookey, 103.

10. Stookey, 25.

11. Lucien Diess, *Springtime of the Liturgy: Liturgical Texts of the First Four Centuries* (Collegeville: The Liturgical Press, 1967).

12. Diess, 23.

13. Ibid.

14. Stookey. This is a summation of the arguments presented in pp. 112-135.

Chapter Ten

Practicing Consensus at the Table
Doing Democracy Differently

Jan Love

> *So then you are no longer strangers and aliens, but you are citizens*
> *with the saints and also members of the household of God, built upon*
> *the foundation of the apostles and prophets, with Christ Jesus himself*
> *as the cornerstone. In him the whole structure is joined together and*
> *grows into a holy temple in the Lord; in whom you also are built*
> *together spiritually into a dwelling place for God. (Eph 2:19-22)*

When we bring our conflicts to the Table, what decision-making process is most appropriate to being the body of Christ? What decision-making process is most conducive to Holy Conferencing? In chapter seven, Tom Porter suggested principles of mediation and restorative justice as guiding principles for how we might practice reconciliation at the Table. These are both consensus processes. He also talked about the possibility of doing decision-making at the Table. This chapter is focused on large group decision-making, which includes dealing with the critical conflictual issues of our day, and will explore the possibilities and promise of developing consensus in our decision-making, whether it be at a church meeting or at general conference. I believe this movement is essential to creating community, practicing Holy Conferencing, living in the Spirit, and being the body of Christ.

Many people in church-related governing bodies want to find a better way of conducting business other than the routine parliamentary procedures that divide people into winners and losers. Skeptics, wary that careful protections guaranteed by such rules and regulations will be lost, express their doubt that church and ecumenical organizations can improve much on a style that has been carefully refined across generations of decision-makers, particularly in Protestant and Anglican arenas.

The World Council of Churches (WCC) Central Committee, the organization's main governing body, decided in 2004 to draft a new set of rules that will govern the organization primarily through consensus methods. If this proves to be a productive course of action, it may have significant consequences for other ecumenical institutions and may even serve as a model for denominations now accustomed to some variation of parliamentary rules of decision making.

This chapter will describe the circumstances that led the WCC to take this historic step, define terms used in the analysis, examine the changes in the WCC Rules of Debate proposed for adoption and implementation at the 2006 Assembly (the WCC's the highest governing body), and discuss the problems anticipated as the process unfolds. I hope this analysis will give some insight into whether this particular ecumenical model holds any lessons and promise for other ecclesial bodies, including my own, the United Methodist Church.

Historical Background: Dealing with Conflict at the Table

The World Council of Churches is the most comprehensive Christian organization in the world. The Council describes itself in promotional material as "the broadest and most inclusive among the many organized expressions of the modern ecumenical movement, a movement whose goal is Christian unity." As of late 2005, it has about 347 member churches from more than 120 countries in all continents. The WCC's members represent about 400 million Christians, including most of the world's Orthodox churches, denominations from historic traditions of the Protestant Reformation such as Anglican, Baptist, Lutheran, Methodist, and Reformed, as well as many united and independent churches. Founded primarily by European and North American churches in 1948, the membership expanded to Africa, Asia, the Caribbean, Latin America, and the Pacific Islands in the 1960s and 1970s as nations in those parts of the world became independent from colonial powers. Now most member churches come from the "south."

The Council's constitution describes its primary goal as "to call one another to visible unity in one faith and in one Eucharistic fellowship, expressed in worship and common life in Christ, through witness and service to the world, and to advance towards that unity in order that the world may believe."

After more than fifty years of governing its life under rules of debate that resemble Robert's Rules of Order, the WCC board of directors, the Central Committee, decided to embrace consensus as the primary mode of decision making. The Council had weathered numerous changes and controversies using parliamentary procedures. The resolve to change came only after three years of careful scrutiny and was one of five key recommendations proposed by the Special Commission on Orthodox Participation in the World Council of Churches. The WCC Eighth Assembly held in Harare, Zimbabwe, in 1998, initiated the Special Commission when representatives of Orthodox churches demanded a re-negotiation of the terms of their participation in the organization.

Many Eastern Orthodox churches endured mounting internal anti-ecumenical pressures after the collapse of communism in Eastern Europe in the late 1980s. The Georgian and Bulgarian Orthodox churches withdrew from WCC membership in 1997. Yet, the WCC continues to be the only arena where Orthodox churches meet each other, as they also encounter Anglican, Lutheran, Reformed, Baptist, Methodist, and other denominations from across the world. Widespread Orthodox dissatisfaction threatened the Council's fellowship and, in many respects, its claim to be the global leader of ecumenism.

Internal tensions facing both the Eastern and Oriental Orthodox churches spurred their leaders to express more sharply and persistently their long-standing theological differences with the organization's Protestant and Anglican majority. Topics that provoke controversy for Orthodox churches such as the ordination of women could be addressed more productively, leaders of these churches asserted, if fundamental changes in decision-making processes were made. They clearly wanted a greater share of power in an institution that had for some decades addressed an expanding agenda that some in the Orthodox traditions found foreign to their understanding of the church.

The Limitations of Robert's Rules of Order

Disaffected constituencies commonly call for changes in how organizations make decisions. As a global institution, the formal rules of the WCC seem foreign to many. Formulated when most of its member churches came from Europe and North America and when governing bodies were overwhelmingly male, some member churches rarely encounter such parliamentary-style politics in their own home settings. Among those that do, many have lamented for years about how such processes force participants into adversarial "yes" and "no" categories when the group often wants to imagine, explore, and discuss alternative possibilities. Although many became adept at using the rules, feminists, young people, and delegates from the Africa, Asia, and Latin America have complained for decades that the WCC rules needed to move away from the model of Western parliaments.

Yet, Western parliaments represent one of the most significant and enduring expressions of democracy in the secular world. Democratic processes, widespread participation in decision-making, and openness to critical feedback do not characterize most ecclesiastical bodies across the globe. In many places, small church hierarchies often make pronouncements that the vast numbers of faithful are expected to swallow whole. For many, opening their churches up to parliamentary-style politics would represent a positive move toward a democratic reformation that is long overdue. Can the World Council of Churches improve on parliamentary procedures that have a significant history of success in both church and secular arenas?

The Promise of Consensus

Some who practice consensus in their own governing bodies answer enthusiastically and emphatically, yes! For example, Eden Grace, a U.S. representative of the Friends (Quakers) in the WCC Central Committee and a member of the Special Commission, argues theologically that "How we make decisions matters, because how we treat each other testifies to whether we are living in the Spirit or not." Our behavior as Christians in governing bodies should reflect "love, respect, and generosity," rather than "suspicion and competition," she says. Many who advocate processes of "discernment" in U.S. churches would agree.

Although he, too, has a theological preference for consensus methods, D'Arcy Wood from the Uniting Church in Australia and a member of the Special Commission makes the case for consensus on more practical grounds. He does so from the experience of his own church that shifted about a decade ago from parliamentary-style methods to consensus. Whether in a small group or an assembly of hundreds, Wood finds democracy to be enhanced considerably in the new procedures, a point the Orthodox find very appealing. Orthodox members of the Special Commission also stated repeatedly that their goal in advocating consensus is primarily practical. They consider themselves to be a permanent minority and feel acutely the danger of being victimized by the tyranny of the majority.

The two Orthodox families hold about twenty-five percent of the seats at the general assemblies and in the on-going governing bodies. The representatives of these churches rarely vote as a bloc in opposition to proposals in governing bodies, but when they do, the occasion is quite memorable because, as with any minority, they typically lose. One clear virtue of consensus is that it protects numeric minorities far better than parliamentary-style rules do. Minority groups, of which Orthodox representatives are only one, will have the right not only to be heard but also to have their opinions formally recorded. Such protection will likely lead the majority to attend more carefully to how minority perspectives might be reflected in the main proposal. If such opinions run completely contrary to the main proposal, the final resolution must register the substance of the dissenting point of view, thereby more accurately recording any significant divisions within the body. If no dissent is recorded, the world will know that a large segment of Christianity is choosing to speak with remarkable cohesion.

I served on the Special Commission and then headed the small group that drafted new procedures for the "Conduct of Meetings," which replaces the old "Rules of Debate." The Special Commission was composed so that it was fifty percent Orthodox representatives, from both the Eastern and Oriental families, and fifty percent representing all the other member churches. Dominated by ordained men from Europe and North America, the Commission had only six women and a small number of lay people, a group completely unlike any other on which I had ever served in WCC arenas.

One of the main Orthodox complaints about the World Council of Churches in recent years has been the role of women. Some of the discussions and debates within the Special Commission grew so deeply and personally offensive to me, I seriously considered resigning. I sought counsel and comfort about my role in the Commission from leaders responsible for ecumenism in the United Methodist Church. I eventually decided to stay, and in my resolve to stay, the recommendation I supported most passionately was the recommendation to move to a consensus model for decision making.

As a woman, I have often found myself in a minority in governing bodies. The protection consensus affords to numerical minorities has the capacity to protect our basic community with each other as Christians, something I found all the more precious when overwhelmed by the perspectives of conscientious people of faith with whom I disagree profoundly on beliefs basic to our common claim to follow Christ. The Special Commission agreed to try to govern itself primarily through consensus. As one who embraced the process, I used consensus procedures repeatedly during the last meeting to incorporate changes in the draft text of the Commission report that I knew would be unacceptable not only to me but also to the United Methodist Church. In the end, the report contained parts with which I disagreed, but the depth and range of my disagreement had become acceptable to me and, I believed, my church.

Democracy and the Meaning of Consensus

So what does consensus mean?

Consensus processes strive to be democratic. Jan Scholte, a scholar of international relations, states that "democracy is understood to prevail when members of a polity determine—collectively, equally and without arbitrarily imposed constraints—the policies that shape their destinies." Democratic decision-making can take many forms, the kind of practices in most of the Western nation-states being just one of many. Whatever form it takes, "in one way or another, democratic governance is participatory, consultative, transparent and publicly accountable"[1]

The kind of democracy that the WCC Central Committee wanted to pursue, according to documents from its September 2003 meeting, would strive:

> to be as simple as possible and only as complex as necessary; to be
> transparent; to enhance participation . . . across the whole group;
> to check the possibility of domination by any participant or small
> group; to manage with courtesy, respect and grace discussions
> where participants bring deeply held, contending perspectives on
> matters at the heart of their Christian convictions; to provide
> orderly deliberations and timely decisions; to explore creative
> alternatives; to check the power of a few participants to obstruct
> decisions when the vast majority is ready to move; to check the
> power of any moderator (chair) to steer the deliberations in
> directions other than those desired by the body; and to
> strengthen the capacity of the churches in fellowship in the
> WCC to engage in common witness and service.[2]

Consensus stands in contrast to parliamentary procedures which are used by a variety of Western-style legislative bodies, including the U.S. Congress. Parliamentary procedures employ motions, amendments, voting, division of the house, minority reports, and other such rules.

In its new procedures, the World Council of Churches defines consensus as:

> a process for seeking the common mind of a meeting without deciding issues by means of voting. A consensus is reached when one of the following occurs: (1) all are in agreement (unanimity); (2) most are in agreement and those who disagree are content that the discussion has been both full and fair and that the proposal expresses the general "mind of the meeting;" the minority therefore gives consent; (3) the meeting acknowledges that there are various opinions, and it is agreed that these be recorded in the body of the proposal . . . ; (4) it is agreed that the matter be postponed; (5) it is agreed that no decision can be reached. Therefore, consensus . . . allows any family or other group of churches . . . to have their objections to any proposal addressed and satisfied prior to the adoption of the proposal.[3]

A variety of techniques are spelled out in the new procedures to determine whether a body, even a group of 1,000 delegates, is moving to consensus. Some safeguards for resorting to voting are included for the extreme cases when consensus might fail. A small set of decisions, like the election of staff, must be made by voting, a provision included to acknowledge that the last two general secretaries were each elected with close to sixty percent of the vote.

In the old style of decision-making, those who knew the rules well had considerable advantage over newcomers or others who might lose track of technicalities. In the new style, insiders are less likely to dominate decisions. In addition, anyone will be able to explore various options on an issue without specifically formulating a motion, an amendment, or an amendment to the amendment. Proposals will be tested and modified by non-binding, "straw votes"—using colored indicator cards or other forms of checking with participants to probe how close the group is to a final resolution.

The moderator (chair) will play a key role in the whole process. He or she must be adept at detecting the "mind" of the meeting, able to help those who require assistance in formulating proposals, and determined to allow a full and fair airing of all relevant viewpoints. Members and leaders of the Central Committee have begun to undertake fairly extensive training to function in the new rules, which may require refinement along the way.

The power of and need for considerable skill in the moderator is one potential danger of consensus methods. Another is a loss of efficiency. Anyone who has witnessed the governing bodies of the WCC can testify, however, that the current rules often fail to maximize productivity. If done well, consensus processes have the potential of lowering confusion and increasing efficiency, especially in comparison to the snarl of parliamentarians debating contending procedural points.

Consensus and Social Justice

The fear most frequently articulated about consensus procedures at Central Committee meetings is that of blunting the cutting edge of controversial stances on public issues or matters of social justice. The WCC has a history of, on occasion, taking stands theologically and politically that some churches or ecumenical groups reach only years later, if then. For example, the WCC engaged in high profile work to abolish apartheid beginning in 1968, and condemned the prosecution of the Gulf War in 1991. Skeptics wonder if consensus methods, with their requirement of listening closely to all opinions, will water down the strength of the Council's prophetic witness. I believe they probably will not.

I served on the WCC Central Committee from 1975 to 1998. For more than fifteen of those years, I chaired one group or another that gave oversight to one or more of the Council's social justice programs, including various public issue committees. One of the strengths of this work has been its pioneering effort to use consensus methods informally, a practice which began before my involvement.

The standard procedure for writing a public issue statement in WCC, for example, is to test text carefully with key affected, often contending, constituencies prior to presenting proposals to formal governing bodies. By the time a document reaches the Executive or Central Committee, it will have been vetted repeatedly with those who have the most at stake. Controversy over public issue statements erupts occasionally on the floor of a meeting, but drafters regularly seek to incorporate concerns as much as possible. Although this process is not perfect, the organization's records demonstrate repeatedly that the statements and programs that outsiders perceive to be the most controversial have almost always been adopted by overwhelming majorities in the governing bodies of the WCC, a situation fairly close to the requirements of consensus methods. Consensus does not have to lead to the lowest common denominator. Historically in its informal use in the Council, a consensus-type process has often led to a powerful public witness.

Consensus, Holy Conferencing, and Holy Communion

Historically, a popular term among Methodists has been holy conferencing. Consensus could facilitate this process, which I view in very practical terms. For me, holy conferencing strives to help everyone recognize the intimate bonds between ends and means. The manner through which we govern our life together in the church profoundly affects the quality of the fellowship we experience and seek together. The means by which we search for a common mind is as important as the decisions we reach. Process matters as much as product or outcome. In all arenas of our life together in the church, even in decision-making arenas, we should seek to build each other up within the body of Christ, to listen carefully to one another's experiences, to intercede on each other's behalf, to speak clearly on common convictions as well as deeply held differences, and thus to grow in faith and in bonds of fellowship. A set of procedures that makes the best possible use of all members' abilities, experiences, commitment, and spiritual strength should be our goal. This spirit is found at the Table of Holy Communion, where we are made "one with Christ, one with each other, and one in ministry to all the world . . . ." Unlike majority votes that divide, exclude and marginalize, consensus recognizes equal voice and participation at the Table. Each part of the body of Christ is essential to the whole. Each is essential to the communal discernment of the guidance of the Spirit, the mind of Christ. Each is essential to our becoming a fellowship of reconciliation at the Table of Reconciliation. With a consensus process we are more likely to name our issues, our harm, and our conflict, as Jesus did. When we work out a consensus, we offer bread to each other.

Conclusion

The WCC already has something of a track record on which to build less adversarial, more democratic methods of decision-making. If it succeeds in this venture of embracing consensus methods as its primary mechanism for governance, perhaps the WCC will demonstrate to churches the world over that doing democracy a bit differently will be practical, productive, and a good way to promote more just and peaceful relations across the Christian family. Moreover, as we work through our conflicts through consensus maybe we will come to some consensus on our shared fellowship at Christ's Table.

Reflection Questions

1. What processes might make it possible for people who disagree deeply to come to a common mind?

2. Is the WCC concept of consensus potentially applicable to groups in which you have participated in making decisions? Why or why not?

3. What does it mean for processes to be as important as products of decision making?

Notes

1. Jan Love, *Southern Africa in World Politics: Local Aspirations and Global Entanglements (Dilemmas in World Politics)* (Boulder: Westview Press, 2005), 108.

2. "Interim Report on Consensus Procedures," World Council of Churches, Central Committee Meeting, Geneva, Switzerland, 26 August–2 September 2003.

3. Ibid.

Chapter Eleven

Gathering at the Roundtable

WILLIAM JOHNSON EVERETT

Twice a month a small group gathers on a Sunday evening in a circle at a round table in the spacious narthex of a church in Waynesville, North Carolina. Songs, readings, prayers, and conversation greet passersby in the hallways, who also see the company sharing bread and passing cups, eating while they talk. Sometimes the speakers pass a feather as they speak in turn. They linger after blessings as they clear the table and return the space to its utilitarian use.

At first glance it may look like just another gathering for prayer, a return to some early form of Methodist class meeting or Moravian love feast, perhaps a house church that has lost its home. In its simplicity it bears these classic marks, but beneath them it is also a hopeful seed of more, even something radical in the original sense. We who gather at the table are seeking the roots of Christian worship in the work of reconciliation as it emerges in the kind of circle processes lifted up in this book. In this brief space I want to make a report from the field about what we do, why we do it, and what we have learned about its challenges.

At the heart of the gathering is the round table. In our time the round table has become a symbol of the revolution from dictatorial or monarchical forms of government to democratic self-government. A "round table" has become a "roundtable." At the roundtable people come together as equals to express and understand their differences, explore their common ground, and negotiate new covenants to shape a new life together in peace. Whether in India's Roundtable Conferences in the early 1930s to find a path to self-governance, in Poland's and East Germany's emergence from Communist rule in the late 1980s, or in many other settings around the world, the roundtable has been both a means to reconciliation and a symbol of non-violent resolution of conflict. As South Africa's Truth and Reconciliation Commission has shown us, the path of negotiated revolution also demands taking the path toward the truth about our brokenness and the reconciliation that can heal us.

The Reasons We Gather

These Sunday evening gatherings are an effort to flesh out a form of worship that puts the dynamic of the roundtable, as a symbol of the work of reconciliation, at its center. The roundtable forms an intersection between the practical effort to transform conflict in our world and the symbolic work of connecting ourselves to the deepest purposes of God—the Holy One who creates, sustains, and transforms our world.

To understand what is going on at the roundtable as a form of worship we need to remember that all worship takes symbols and practices from our social and political life in order to connect us to the deepest patterns and energies of existence.[1] Whether it employs the kneeling and clasped hands that bound vassals to lords in medieval Europe, or the ecstatic waving hands of a rock concert, worship both borrows from its cultural environment and also gives back symbols and rituals that it has baptized in transcendent meanings. The question for worship leaders has always been what cultural symbols and practices to borrow, how to reconstruct them within a theological framework, and how to re-introduce them to the environing culture. Roundtable-centered worship is no exception.

As I look at it, roundtable worship makes the most sense if we look at worship first of all as a kind of drama. Vital worship is the rehearsal of a primordial drama that we enter in order to find a meaningful place in the narrative of human life. Worship is an ever-repeated but always changing theatrical reality that gives us roles, scripts, plots, and properties for living out our lives. In this sense the roundtable can be seen as a theatrical property that stands at the center of a drama of reconciliation. The drama it evokes, however, is not the only form that the drama of reconciliation has taken in Christian churches over the centuries. While the drama of the roundtable reaches back to the earliest elements of Jewish and Christian understandings of reconciliation, it stands in sharp tension with what has been the dominant worship drama of reconciliation—the drama of the sacrifice of the Son to the Father.

This sacrificial drama focuses on the altar. It presents reconciliation within a hierarchical relationship, especially that of patriarchal hierarchy. The altar sees reconciliation as the result of a once-bloody sacrifice of an obedient son to his father. This self-sacrificing obedience encapsulated the core issues of how power and authority are transmitted from the patriarch to his son, who must be obedient in order to inherit the kingdom of his father. This was the political vision at the heart of the Christian worship that built on the story of Abraham's willingness to sacrifice Isaac, on the Psalms of King David, on Isaiah's prophecies, and on the life of Jesus. It finds its most elaborate rehearsal in the rituals of Holy Week.

The roundtable sees reconciliation as a new relationship among women and men who have been baptized into the equality of a new assembly. While the altar focuses on obedience, the table lifts up persuasion, mutual empathy, and the dynamics of circle process explored by Thomas Porter and Marcia McFee in this book. At the table, reconciliation emerges in the meeting, eating, and conversing together at table. In the biblical narrative we see it emerging in the reversal of roles at Holy Thursday, in the disciples' resurrection encounters with the Christ as they break bread, and in the language-transcending communication at Pentecost. Reconciliation requires that the conversation evoked at the table culminate in a renewed covenant to seek right relationships with each other and with God's creation. The covenant that emerges at the traditional altar is a hierarchical covenant offered by a king to his vassal. The covenant emerging at the table is one of mutual promise among fellow citizens gathered in the Spirit of the Christ, that is, the Spirit of a coming new creation.

The gathering in a circle around the Table is a powerful symbol of this work of reconciliation, mutual responsibility, and renewed commitment to the common good. The circle processes embedded in Native American tradition, in nineteenth century women's circles, in councils and negotiations among equals since time immemorial are remembered and rehearsed in our circle gathering.[2]

The roundtable stands not only at the intersection of the practical work of reconciliation and the symbolic work of worship. It also forms a kind of meeting place between the sacramental traditions of worship centered in the altar, and preaching traditions centered in the pulpit. Sacramentalists, as in the worship reforms after the Second Vatican Council, have increasingly refocused worship on the table. At the same time churches rooted in a preaching tradition have begun placing the table at least on an equal plane with the pulpit. The roundtable seeks to transform both the content of sacramental worship as well as the meaning of "the Word" uttered from the pulpit. Just as it moves the work of reconciliation from the altar of sacrifice to the table of negotiation, so the roundtable shifts the meaning of "the Word" from the one-way commands of a single authority to a conversation among the many. In theological terms it takes seriously that "the Word," the "logos" of God, is constituted in a Trinitarian conversation represented by the whole assembly rather than simply in the Christ figure, represented in a clergy person.[3]

Our Roundtable Experience

These are some of the reasons why we gather at the roundtable in the way that we do. Now let me walk you through a typical gathering at our own roundtable to present things more concretely. Along the way I will give my own interpretation of these actions, though others at the table would want to enter a conversation about them as well!

Setting the table is a very important part of the gathering. When appropriate, a tablecloth is selected that dramatizes or highlights the anticipated focus of conversation. We often use a multi-pattern cloth to symbolize the variety of people and concerns that are coming to the table. A candle is always present to symbolize the search for a common light of wisdom to illuminate our conversation. Sometimes it is circled by barbed wire, as with the logo for Amnesty International, to symbolize the bondage and alienation oppressing people and other creatures of the earth. Some connection to the earth, whether by water, soil, or plants, almost always figures in the setting, reminding us of the ecological dimension to God's creative work and every human act. A feather, often used in Native American circles, usually lies on the table to remind us of the precious privilege and invitation to speak and to listen respectfully to the other. Breadstuff and drink, sometimes with other food, completes the setting.

Our speaking begins with a call to the table. We begin with words of invitation and response, as with Jesus' own parables of banquets (Luke 14:15-24; Matthew 22:1-14; cf. Proverbs 9:1-6). The call often reminds us of our alienation, brokenness, isolation, and fear as well as the goodness and the bounty waiting at God's welcome table.

The songs we use are simple and singable, with guitar accompaniment or a cappella. We are committed to using language that truly invites all people to the table, regardless of all the divisions and categories of separation among us.[4] In doing this, we seek a language and symbols that express the holiness of a God beyond sex, gender, and other human conventions. In keeping with the dynamics of roundtable reconciliation we often employ images of God's wisdom, love, patience, listening, and creative reconciliation. One of our biggest challenges is in employing the language of governance appropriate to the roundtable—such as democracy, constitution, republic, or covenant—without reducing God's coming creation to our own preconceptions of ultimate order, justice, and peace. In any event, we try to avoid speaking as if we were fifteenth-century monarchists! Our language is always a struggle to hold together our human aspirations with God's amazing future.

Having accepted the call to the table, we move to an affirmation of God's goodness and care. We begin by remembering the divine work of reconciliation in the past. The events we recall, whether in biblical history or other events, stand forth as promissory intimations of the table dynamic of reconciliation as it might be present in this gathering. We then give thanks, the human acknowledgement of the goodness of God. We start here, not with God's omnipotent loftiness and our unworthiness, but simply with the beauty, sustenance, and creative kindness that in fact has sustained us to this day. Coming to the table is not an act of penitence, as it has been so often in Christian history, but a joyful response to the goodness of God's open invitation. The table is not the reward for worthiness dispensed to those who are in good standing, but an evocation of gratitude and a sense of humility that leads us to an exploration of how we can extend God's goodness in our life.[5]

The serving and sharing of food and drink is somewhat informal. We often talk as we eat about the meaning of this meal action on this particular evening, some-times recalling stories, sometimes other associations in our minds from Scripture, literature, songs, or recent events. People are invited to continue eating and sipping throughout our subsequent conversation. It is in this synergy of nurture and con-versation that we live into and live out the "Holy Communion" by which these acts have been identified in Christian history.

The conversation we then enter is introduced by a reading, usually from Scrip-ture, to focus our thoughts. We have entertained and continue to keep open the possibility that dance, visual art, or some other presentation could also initiate our way into conversation, but our abilities have not yet extended that far. Each evening a conversation moderator introduces the focus and guides the conversation, some-times using the feather to elicit remarks from everyone who wants to speak. Some-times tears are evoked, as when we voiced lament for the sufferings of children, or when people gained the courage to share festering pains, as in an exploration of the church's struggle with sexual orientation. There is often laughter. The sharing of words in this context is more than a transmission of information; it is a form of commitment to each other that clarifies as it respects differences, while at the same time affirming common ground. It is in the conversation and our prayers that we often plumb the awareness that our own acts and the world we know do not reflect fully the goodness God has intended in creation.

Conversation at table requires that we sit in a circle facing one another. This produces a very different energy from the customary form of audience seating. This is not merely a matter of comfortable intimacy, but a sense of shared participation in a dynamic that emerges from our focus on the common table and all that it sym-bolizes. In facing the common table we also sense a mutual accountability and col-laboration in a common work as well as in celebration.

The conversation leads to speech in prayer, essentially direct address to the God who creates and reconciles our world. It expands the conversation, not only by direct address to the Holy One who listens, but also by explicit reference to people, creatures, and conditions beyond our little circle. In prayer we expand our little cir-cle to the great circle of the universe. For many of our members this action reflects a deep struggle to escape postures of childish request, magical solicitation, and "talk-ing to the ceiling," as we probe more deeply into the conversation that participates in the healing of the world. The prayers lead into what we call the Hope Prayer, which is a fresh expression of the model prayer Jesus taught his disciples. We have modified it over time. Here is its current expression:

> O Source of Life,
> You alone are holy.
> Come and govern us in perfect peace.
> Give us today all the food that we need.
> Release us from sin as we release our enemies.
> Save us in the trials of judgment.

Liberate us all from evil powers.
For in you is our justice,
Our constitution, and our peace. AMEN.

We then conclude with some act of commitment that binds us into this hoped-for future. It is a time of covenant or re-covenanting, in which the work of reconciliation always has to eventuate and which sets the standard of accountability for the future. This culminates in a blessing which we speak or sing to one another, often accompanied by some ritual sign, such as in the "Indonesian handshake" taught to us by one of our members, in which we place our hand over our heart as well as in the hands of the other.

Findings and Challenges

What, then, have we found in this roundtable worship experience? What have we learned from these experiments? Some participants have said that the language and symbols we use at table open up a way out of an oppressive and stifling religious past. Other participants have discovered unexpected wisdom or perspectives in the conversation that enrich their lives. The conversation enables them both to bring concerns from their world to the table and take away some shared insight or commitment. For some, simply being in circle around the roundtable, with its evocative setting, leaves them with a new sense of depth or wholeness. They experience both a seriousness and a refreshing lightness at the same time, as they share burdens and joys.

The roundtable requires shared leadership that rotates among the participants according to their gifts and abilities. Different people lead the circle in liturgy, meal, conversation, prayer, and song. The worship focuses on what is symbolized by the table rather than on a particular leader. Similarly, what would usually be a statement by one person becomes a conversation among many. In all these ways, people are drawn from passivity to active participation.

Our exploration thus far has also posed at least five challenges. First is the question of size. While we have remained a small group, we ask ourselves how would a larger group still maintain the essentials of the roundtable experience? I think that the main change would be for the conversation to become a "representative" experience, in which a panel or dialogue would represent the conversation of the whole assembly. What would be crucial is that, through portable microphones or other means, the word as dialogue would be preserved. In this sense, the televised town meeting offers a model. Worship, as a longing for the full realization of our ethical yearnings, would still point to a pattern of communication in which all participate.

The question of scale is also related to the question of where we should gather: in a "sacred space"? in a church? in a public building or storefront? Since most (but not all!) of our churches are designed like shoeboxes or fans so that one person can speak to the many, it is difficult to find a sanctuary that echoes our commitment to circular process. However, it is clear that whatever space we meet in has to be hospitable to the spirituality that undergirds and emanates from the roundtable. Each roundtable group would have to resolve this significant challenge in its own way.

The second challenge remains that of developing a language and symbolism that moves us fully from the models of patriarchy, monarchy, and outmoded cosmologies to those of democratic participation dependent on the earth's delicate ecology in an expanding universe. We continue to experiment, as so many others do, with language, symbolism, and rituals that can meet this challenge within the context of our gathering at table.

The third challenge lies in the realization that this kind of worship requires not only group planning but also personal development and formation. Every form of worship requires some sort of training among the worshippers, even if it is to discipline them to silence and sitting. The roundtable form, like the exercise of citizenship in a democracy, requires training in self-expression, attentive listening, patient self-restraint, and the habit of reflecting on our actions. It requires a deeper knowledge of Scripture, Christian tradition, human wisdom, and awareness of what is going on in the world if one is to share in a way helpful to others. Every developed form of worship faces similar challenges, but we sense them more in recovering and developing this particular form.

The fourth challenge is to pursue and maintain the diversity that makes reconciliation and conversation both necessary and possible.[6] Not only do we face the challenge of forming people with the manners of this peculiar table, but of enabling people with diverse beliefs, backgrounds, opinions, perspectives, and experiences to come to the table. In our own world it is a daunting challenge to enable people to lay down their means of violence to come to the table of persuasion. In some ways it is no less a challenge to maintain the diversity that leads both to fearful violence and to mutual enrichment.

The fifth challenge is to address more effectively and creatively the connection between our symbolic actions of worship and our actual practices of reconciliation in the church and in wider publics. While our regular gatherings always take up specific issues and conflicts needing healing and reconciliation, the form of our worship makes it difficult for reconciliation to occur in specific ways in that setting. Such a process would probably exceed the time limits we have set for our worship gathering. In addition, the practical work of reconciliation in specific cases may well have more stringent rules of confidentiality and participation. Moreover, unless the conflict emerges from within the community gathered at the table, the worshipping group is usually not the same as the web of relationships in which our conflicts emerge. Thus, we have encountered a number of practical sources for the distinction between our symbolic actions of ordinary worship and the actual work of conflict transformation and reconciliation in specific cases.

Nevertheless, our worship gatherings are times when we lay down, like a deep bedrock, the foundations for reconciliation processes in our church and other churches as well as in our wider community. Through symbols and rituals, worship explicitly immerses us in the common waters from which spring the energies and patterns of reconciliation. It forms us as persons and groups. It shapes our dispositions, sensitivities, and habits of response. It provides scripts with which we move into the wider drama of our lives. Through the actions of worship, we link our own yearnings to the ultimate purposes of God. Worship presents the dramatic form at the core of reconciliation, even when it does not complete an actual healing encounter in a particular context of need.

Within our own wider congregation the roundtable has been a place where people have come to deal with actual issues of racism, conflicts over homosexuality, responses to hurricane disasters, evolution, and many other conflicts around us. Our gatherings have a ripple effect in the wider congregation. We are now engaged in seeking ways to carry this roundtable dynamic into the life of the church in more explicit ways, such as those described by Thomas Porter earlier in this volume. Within the church community, this kind of worship setting can function, we believe, to enable us to grapple with contentious issues that are too hot to handle from the pulpit or in traditional ways of meeting and decision-making.

Seeking to engage issues beyond the congregation, we have brought into our conversations local leaders in mediation work, in controversies embedded in racial discrimination, or in struggles for quality education for our children. We see their work as anchored deeply in the core dynamics of reconciliation rehearsed regularly in our worship gatherings. Knowing that their work is anchored in their own faith traditions can help strengthen and guide them. We are still struggling with ways to support them more directly, even though they operate in a milieu that is not explicitly religious. Our roundtable worship continually invites and urges us to find ways to extend the roundtable dynamic into the wider community.

In spite of these challenging gaps, the two activities of roundtable worship and of conflict transformation are deeply connected, because, we believe, they participate in the one reconciling work of the Creator of all. They are two inseparable though distinct dimensions of the reconciliation process. Worship is an energizing source, a grounding of our lives in the historical drama of reconciliation that takes place in specific contexts in a language of the place and people in conflict. The work of conflict transformation in specific situations stands at the heart of what the reconciliation rehearsed in worship is all about. Reconciliation in these particular contexts yields explicitly religious meanings, just as worship has a particular "address" at the doorstep of everyday life. The challenge we face is finding creative ways to relate them to each other more dynamically.

The roundtable is a struggling and delicate seedling in our midst, but it is also rooted in deep and ancient soils fed by biblical accounts, historical experience, and our contemporary yearnings for a world of democratic participation, reconciliation, and ecological responsibility. For it to become a tree that can give us shade, nurture, and protection we must continue in our husbandry. Perhaps, as the book of Revelation says, it can become a tree whose "leaves . . . are for the healing of the nations."

Reflection Questions

1. What drama of reconciliation is being presented in your current worship form and setting? How does it reflect the way conflicts are dealt with in your church and community? What drama of reconciliation might speak more deeply to your community?

2. Are there any places in your church life or community where roundtable dynamics are occurring? How might your worship expand and deepen them?

Notes

1. See my book *The Politics of Worship: Reconstructing the Language and Symbols of Worship* (Cleveland: United Church Press, 1999). For additional pertinent perspectives see Tom F. Driver, *The Magic of Ritual: Our Need for Liberating Rites that Transform Our Lives and Our Communities* (San Francisco: Harper, 1991).

2. For an extensive exploration of circle dynamics in this respect see Kay Pranis, Barry Stuart, and Mark Wedge, *Peacemaking Circles: From Crime to Community* (St. Paul: Living Justice Press, 2003).

3. For an expansion of this theme see Lucy Rose Atkinson, *Sharing the Word: Preaching in the Roundtable Church* (Louisville: Westminster/John Knox, 1997).

4. Among the many contributions to this effort, see Ruth C. Duck, *Gender and the Name of God: The Trinitarian Baptismal Formula* (New York: Pilgrim, 1991); Gail Ramshaw, *Reviving Sacred Speech: The Meaning of Liturgical Language* (Akron: OSL Publications, 2000) and Brian Wren, *What Language Shall I Borrow? GodTalk in Worship: A Male Response to Feminist Theology* (New York: Crossroads, 1989).

5. The shift in the meaning of the table from that of penitent self-sacrifice to that of fellowship with God and anticipation of God's future has been nurtured by many people. For a recent statement see, June Christine Goudey, *The Feast of our Lives: Re-imaging Communion* (Cleveland: Pilgrim Press, 2002).

6. A number of theologians and worship leaders struggle with this issue in Brian Blount and Leonora Tubbs Tisdale, eds., *Making Room at the Table: An Invitation to Multicultural Worship* (Louisville: Westminster/John Knox, 2001).

Conclusion

Breaking Down the Walls and Coming to the Table

In seminary, I interned at Salem United Methodist Church in Harlem. Roy Nichols, who became a bishop in the United Methodist Church, was the pastor. On Worldwide Communion Sunday, the matriarch of the church, during Holy Communion, went to each of the walls of the church and pounded on them saying, "We need to break down the walls of this church so that everyone can come to the Table of our Lord." This Table is not only for our church, but it is also for the communities and the world in which we live.

This is the dream we have for the Table! When people walk by your church, you hear them say: "Inside this church is a Table. It is a healing, restoring Table. At this Table, you truly hear and experience the "good news" of God's love and forgiveness. You also find people living out the call to a ministry of reconciliation. Here is a place where you can be authentic, including dealing with your hurt and your conflicts. Here conflicts are named, but not in the spirit of punishment, but in the spirit of getting to a good place together. My friend came to a good place with his family at this Table. Another friend came to a good place with his neighbor with whom he had been feuding. Folks gather around this Table to discuss the major issues of the day and to discern what God's love is calling us to do. This Table has become the center every Sunday of weekly celebrations of restoration, healing, and reconciliation. Everything becomes "new" at this table. I want to be a part of this place with this Table."

Is this more than a dream? The contributors to this book believe that it is more than possible, that it is our calling, that it has been experienced, and that it is essential to the future of the church and the world.

The words of the contributors express this best. At this Table, as we deeply remember and internalize the actions of Jesus at the Last Supper of naming and giving bread, we break the cycles of punishment, retribution, and violence and "re-member or re-frame our world and our own actions." We realize that "it is only through divine grace that conflicts can be mediated, forgiveness granted, and rec-onciliation actualized in our world." We become the "beloved community." "We embrace and offer forgiveness as the incomparable gift it is." We are formed into peacebuilders. With Ike Moloabi and his Afrikaner guard, we affirm that "commun-ion is a converting ordinance and when the church is willing to trust what this table can do, people change." Here we demonstrate our faithfulness as "we engage ritual practices of naming conflict, and breaking bread in the midst of these 'deep things.'" Our learnings from the field of conflict transformation will reach a new depth as we bring our conflicts to the Table.

"In the practice of Holy Communion, we open ourselves to the living and heal-ing presence of God and to the imaginative possibilities of the fullness of God's restoration and *shalom*." "At the end of the day, the Eucharist is a celebration of table fellowship which foretells of the lavish welcome that God has prepared for us as a beloved community. The bread and the wine are our soul's food." At the Table, we will realize that "the means by which we search for a common mind is as impor-tant as the decisions we reach." We come away from the Table, ideally a roundtable, having "discovered unexpected wisdom or perspectives in the conversation," "shared insight or commitment," "a new sense of depth or wholeness," and "both a serious-ness and a refreshing lightness."

Steps for Conflict Transformation

Prepare Yourself for Conflict Transformation

CREATE A WELL, NOT A WALL
Create in yourself an openness to conflict as part of God's creation,
an opportunity for growth and revelation.

ALLOW THE WELL TO FILL
Open your heart and mind to God's love, as incarnate in Jesus the Christ,
reducing your anxiety and drawing you toward reconcilliation and
being a reconciler.

BE WELL PREPARED
Be prepared to listen for understanding, speak the truth in love,
use your imagination, and be forgiving.

BE WELL
Accept forgiveness and healing so that you can be a mediative
presence in the conflict.

Engage Others in Conflict Transformation

CREATE A COMMON WELL TOGETHER
Together analyze the conflict and design a collaborative process
where everyone can participate and be responsible.

SHARE THE WELL
Create a relational covenant that clarifies and affirms how everyone
will be treated in the process.

Drink Deeply Together
Elicit stories of peak experiences, grace-filled moments, and dreams
of a preferred future.

Let It Flow
Move from positions to interests and needs, generating options to reach consensus. Move from retribution to restoration: healing the harm, affirming
accountability, and creating a new relationship.

Be Well Together
Celebrate each step toward healing and communion.
Be prayerful, persistent, and patient.